Pope John Paul II
and the Luminous Mysteries
of the Rosary

Pope John Paul II
and the
Luminous Mysteries
of the Rosary

By
Jerome M. Vereb, C.P.

CATHOLIC BOOK PUBLISHING CO.
New Jersey

NIHIL OBSTAT: Hugh Eamon McManus, S.T.D.
Censor Librorum

IMPRIMATUR: ✠ The Most Rev. Norbert M. Dorsey, C.P., S.T.D.
Bishop of Orlando

> Every dawn renews the Beginning, and to behold the earth struggling out of the formless void, out of the night, is to witness the act of creation. *Sholem Asch*

This book has been published by arrangement with The K.S. Giniger Company, Inc., 250 West 57 Street, Suite 414, New York, NY 10107.

(T-118)

Dedicated to the memory of my parents,

Joseph Vincent Vereb (1912-1963)

and

Helen Larner Vereb (1912-1987)

Acknowledgments

In the preparation of this book, I am particularly grateful to Andrew G. Wilson, who has faithfully stayed at my side through the research, composition, and editing, which was compacted into several rather intense weeks. I also express gratitude to Father Xavier Hayes, C.P., who is ever faithful in providing resources. It was my pastor, the late Father John C. Fallon (1877-1955), who taught me to love the Rosary. He is now long deceased, but it is my prayer that his memory be eternal. My thanks also go to Father Michael C. MacVeigh and Monsignor Joseph Findlan of the Diocese of Pittsburgh and Monsignor George Coyne of the Diocese of Steubenville, who had a profound effect on my vocation to the priesthood. Finally, I am grateful to my cousins, Margaret Rose, Dorothy, and Loretta Vereb, who, as always, have been very supportive.

Contents

PART II: THE LUMINOUS MYSTERIES OF POPE JOHN PAUL II

Preface

THE promulgation of the Apostolic Letter, *Rosarium Virginis Mariae*, by Pope John Paul II on October 16, 2002, comes as a welcome surprise to the entire Church. By addressing devotion to the Rosary of the Blessed Virgin Mary, the Holy Father has chosen to thus inaugurate the Silver Jubilee Year of his Pontificate. Not only has he identified the power of the prayer of the Rosary, but he has added a new series of Mysteries of the Rosary known as the Luminous Mysteries. In so doing, he has broken precedent. Not only has he expanded the number of Mysteries from 15 to 20, but he has focused more directly on the Public Life of Jesus and His message.

This innovation provides a remarkable pastoral tool through which it is possible to acknowledge the content of Jesus' public preaching and ministry. In particular, the central teaching of Jesus, the "Kingdom of God," calls for renewed pastoral examination. Ours is an age of both rapid social change and an obviously deepening commitment to material and secular aspirations toward success, privilege, power, and acquisition. According to New Testament Apocalyptic teaching, these are hallmarks of the kingdom of Satan, whose principal representative on this earth, the devil, attempts to seduce the elect to turn and worship the Beast. The kingdom of this world masquerades much privilege and possessions as a god. Jesus, by proclaiming that the Name of the

Father *is* hallowed, inaugurates the *true* Kingdom. Through His Public Life, Jesus is completely identified with God as His Father and with God's future, where all of the baptized are called to stand among the elect; they have a place in the Kingdom of God, which is beginning even now.

The *Luminous Mysteries* also highlight the Institution of the Eucharist, making it the central Mystery of the Holy Rosary. It is my view that by this gesture Pope John Paul II is affirming that the tradition of the Rosary is linked with the celebration of the Eucharist, and is, in its own way, a part of the Prayer of the Church. I have observed this fact to be verified by the practice of the many faithful of my diocese. Daily, large groups of people gather in parishes throughout Orlando to pray the Rosary before or after the celebration of the daily Mass, making it a part of the daily ritual of Eucharistic praise and thanksgiving.

By presenting the events of the lives of Jesus and Mary in such innovative fashion, Pope John Paul II has called for a re-examination of all devotion in light of the richness of Sacred Scripture. In the early days of the Church, it was recognized that the inspired texts and documents were themselves a source of grace. They were then known as "the Books." Later, they were called "the Bible," which means "the books put together." When read alongside one another, both Old and New Testaments provide a richness of experience and understanding which enhances the practice of the faith. We live in an age afflicted with "biblical illiteracy." The recitation of the Rosary, according to the method suggested by Pope John Paul II, encourages deeper familiarity with the Scriptures and enhances the desire to study and imbibe them.

I welcome the publication of Father Jerome Vereb's new book, *Pope John Paul II and the Luminous Mysteries of the Rosary,* and hope that you will derive from it understanding and insight. May Our Lady of the Rosary accompany your reading and prayers and be a source of blessing.

Most Reverend Norbert M. Dorsey, C.P., S.T.D.
Bishop of Orlando
December 8, 2002

Introduction

THIS work comes from a series of personal experiences in the recent years of my priestly life. One of these was on Good Friday morning, 2000, when I slipped into a monastery church in the city of Valetta, Malta, in order to attend the Office of Tenebrae as chanted by the Franciscan Friars. Without knowing it, I found myself near the tomb of a much revered Maltese hero, Father George Preca (1880-1962), whose monument, even in that somber atmosphere of Passiontide, was decorated with roses, lilies, and olive branches.

I had come over from Rome to Malta in order to make a Holy Week retreat. I did so by celebrating the Sacred Triduum Services with the Dominican Community in Valetta at St. Dominic's Priory as well as by participating in the extraordinary Holy Week processions of statues and scenes from the Passion Narrative of our Divine Savior. The celebrations were undertaken by the entire Island; thus I found myself passing from church to church for various ceremonies during the day.

Night after night during Holy Week, lifelike images of the Sorrowful Mysteries of the Rosary, carved in heavy types of wood, such as mahogany and oak, were carried through the streets, hoisted on the shoulders of muscular young men who had previously thrown dice in order to "win" the privilege of "bearing the mystery," e.g., the Agony in the Garden, the Scourging at the Pillar, the Way of the Cross, etc.

Holy Week in the city of Valetta, and indeed throughout the nation of Malta, is such a unique experience,
because the entire island is Christian and the celebration of the Redemption—Christ's Passion, Death,
and Resurrection—invites universal participation
there.

The cities and towns are lighted nightly by candles and torches. Young and old line the streets,
singing hymns and praying the Rosary, sounding
bells and shooting off cannons. This medieval tradition carries straight through Holy Week into Easter
Week, when the processions of Lent give way to the
Paschal motif. This time the Glorious Mysteries of the
Rosary are represented. As an American priest and
pilgrim, I was truly moved and renewed by this public display of the significance of the Rosary, obvious
proof of the unbroken continuation of the piety of the
Pilgrim People of God which began there in the
Middle Ages.

As I knelt next to the tomb of Father George
Preca, I saw that he was indeed a beloved and important figure in the legend of Malta, already so rich in
Christian history through the presence of the Order of
the Knights of St. John from the sixteenth century.
Father Preca was a humble Maltese priest of the twentieth century who spent his time catechizing the youth
of Malta. He wandered through Valetta's many ports
attempting to bring the Gospel to tourists, naval personnel, and merchant marine sailors who docked
there for a time and who, during their recreation peri-
ods, often visited Malta's many baroque churches.

Here, statues of the Mysteries of the Rosary were housed in the various niches in the nave when they were not on procession. Father Preca used these carved figures of the Mysteries of the Rosary to explain to visitors and tourists the events of the life of Christ, the salvation through Jesus'blood on the Cross, and the significance and comfort of the Rosary itself. In 1957, Father Preca began to make personal use of five new Mysteries of the Rosary which he called *"Mysteries of Light"* or the Luminous Mysteries. He shared them with colleagues and friends.

Given the specific atmosphere and culture in which Father Preca lived and carried on his ministry, it is not surprising that the five new Mysteries which he felt inspired to publish were called *Mysteries of Light*. During the Paschaltide processions through the narrow streets of Valetta, the total darkness of that Mediterranean island was dispelled by the bright torches which preceded the statues. His devotion of the new *Mysteries of Light* centered around the events of Jesus' Public Life, and were intended to draw the devotee closer to Christ, both in his person and in his mission. Seemingly, this private devotion of the"luminous"*Mysteries of the Rosary* reached the desk of Pope John Paul II sometime before he beatified George Preca of Malta in the year 2001.

This new expression of devotion became public and universal with the Apostolic Letter of Pope John Paul II of October 16, 2002, entitled *Rosarium Virginis Mariae* ("The Rosary of the Virgin Mary"). As he signed the document, Pope John Paul II noted in the letter that the date, October 16, was the twenty-fourth anniversary of his own election as Pope; it was the beginning of his Silver Jubilee Year as Supreme Pontiff of the Roman Catholic Church. Therefore, the Pope noted: "The Rosary, though clearly Marian in character, is at heart a Christocentric prayer. In the sobriety of its elements, it has all the depth of the Gospel message in its entirety of which it can be said to be a compendium" (*Rosarium Virginis Mariae*, hereafter *RVM*, no. 1).

The emphasis on the life of Christ, in terms of His Public Ministry, is a response to a need long expressed by Roman Catholic theologians for greater devotional attention to the events of the life of Jesus between the Incarnation and the Redemption. The Creed has traditionally and consistently professed: *"Jesus Christ, born of the Virgin Mary, suffered under Pontius Pilate, was crucified, died, and was buried. He descended into hell and on the third day He rose again from the dead. . . ."* In the past century and a half, theologians such as Johann Adam Möhler, John Henry Cardinal Newman, Karl Adam, Karl Rahner, S.J., Edward Schillebeeckx, O.P., Gerald O'Collins, S.J., Christoph Cardinal von Schönbron, O.P., Walter Cardinal Kasper, and Avery Cardinal Dulles, S.J., have expressed the need not to allow the phraseology of the Creed to appear as a *lacuna* either in the contemporary study of Christology or in the modern devotional life of the Church!

The need for reemphasis upon Christocentric devotional prayer has been consistent with a reemphasis upon the content of Jesus' Public Ministry by theologians and biblical scholars alike. This has become particularly acute in the mid-twentieth century when rampant secularism, even paganism, found expression, not only in Nazism, Fascism, and Communism but also in a *laissez-faire* kind of relativism that arose from the shards and ruins of the Second World War. Some countries, cultures, and individuals have succumbed to nihilism. Alas, such an attitude, worldly in character, persists today, and sadly it is accompanied by a noticeable lack of attention on the part of the clergy to the Church's devotional life.

Many Catholics complain that devotional services have either been truncated or dismissed altogether and that sermons from the altar certainly do not incite such piety. The hunger is for knowledge of the person of Jesus and His times, and a felt desire to experience the presence of God. For these pastoral reasons as well as from the discipline of biblical studies, such opinions have been reinforced by contemporary Bible scholars, such as Augustin Cardinal Bea, S.J., Archbishop John Whealon, Barnabas Mary Ahern, C.P., Joseph Fitzmyer, S.J., Raymond Brown, S.S., Brendan Byrne, S.J., and Donald Senior, C.P., all of whom have reflected continuing developments in the important area of the study of Sacred Scripture and their application to the faith-life of the community, the family, and the individual.

Since the Christological debates at the time of the Council of Nicea (325 C.E.), the place of Christ in liturgical prayer—i.e., the celebration of Mass and the Sacraments, and later the observance of the Breviary—has been the focus of the Church's daily life of prayer and worship. It has pervaded the Sacred Seasons and the Feasts throughout the Church's Calendar. In the Liturgy, Christ's presence is adored and direct recognition is given to His glory in the Most Blessed Trinity, where Jesus Himself is seen as priest and the mediator of prayer, worship, and contemplation before the Father, in the power of the Holy Spirit.

Most especially, in the twentieth century, from a time preceding the Second Vatican Council (1962-1965), liturgical scholars have continually reemphasized the role of Christ as Lord, priest, and mediator. Scholars such as Josef Jungmann, Lambert Beauduin, O.S.B., Jean Cardinal Daniélou, S.J., Virgil Michel, O.S.B., Dame Aemiliana Lohr, O.S.B., and Louis Bouyer, C.O., dedicated their academic lives to demonstrating this theological insight and dogma for the lives of all the Pilgrim People of God. This point became highlighted under the title of "the Royal Priesthood of Christ" in the documents of the Second Vatican Council.

A pastoral problem faces the Church. Since the dawn of this new millennium, which has carried over from the last century a religious indifferentism in and among the nations of the West and, at the same time, brought heightened attention to religious and political turmoil in the Middle East, so well epitomized in the shock waves sent around the world by the events of September 11, 2001, the patent need is to address the question of the significance of Jesus for *all* of humanity. It is a fact that religion is at the heart of current cultural, economic, and political interaction. Some scholars speak of a global religious destiny which cites Abraham, Moses, Mohammed, and the Buddha, along with Jesus, as merely "the great prophets!" Along with these academics, they declare that, like Gandhi, Jesus represents the best of humanity's potential.

However, the Bible, the Revealed Word of God, delineates the specificity and uniqueness of the person of Jesus. The Gospel writers declare that the Christ-event is the divine disclosure of Jesus as the Son of the Father, the Messiah and the fullness of Revelation. The New Testament, principally in the Pauline texts, contains the biblical significance of "soteriology," the pledge of eternal life given to each of Christ's disciples. This is symbolized by the multiple expressions of the term *basileia*—"the Kingdom of God." According to this principle of Eschatology, found explicitly in the writings of Paul, Mark, Matthew, and Luke, and analogically in John, "now" *(kairos)* is transformed because of Christ's presence among us as Lord *(kyrios)*. This has become known as *Cosmic Redemption*.

After all, the first profession of the Christian Creed was, in fact, that Jesus Christ is Lord: ". . . so that at the name of Jesus *(To onomati Iesou)* every knee should bend in heaven and on earth . . . and every tongue should confess that Jesus Christ is Lord *(Iesous Christos)* to the glory of God the Father *(eis doxan Theou Patros)*" (Phil 2:10-11). This primitive expression of Christian belief is a hymn from the early Galilean *"Followers of the Name."* From the start, the Christian religious recognized and announced that the Christ is the continual living link between heaven and earth.

This insight is derived from the events of Jesus' Public Life and preaching as recorded by John the Evangelist and the Synoptic writers, Matthew, Mark, and Luke. It is the consistent and dominating theme of the Pauline preaching. Recent discoveries of and renewed appreciation for Apocryphal writings, such as the gospels of Thomas, Peter, and Jude, and the newly intensified study of the Apostolic Fathers, including Ignatius of Antioch, Polycarp of Smyrna, Clement of Rome, and the *Shepherd of Hermas,* renew the significance of the Kingdom of God. Now, by promulgating the events of the ministry of Jesus in a new set of decades, termed the *Luminous Mysteries of the Rosary,* Pope John Paul II has acknowledged this truth: *"Each of these mysteries is a revelation of the Kingdom, now present in the very person of Jesus"* (RVM, no. 21).

Pope John Paul II, therefore, announced the following as accurately representing the content of Jesus' words and deeds in the course of His Public Ministry: (1) His Baptism in the Jordan, (2) His Self-manifestation at the wedding at Cana, (3) His proclamation of the Kingdom of God (also found to be at the heart of the Lord's Prayer) and His call to inner renewal which heralded the invitation to conversion *(metanoia),* (4) His transfiguration, and finally (5) His institution of the Eucharist as the Sacramental expression *(mysterion)* of the Paschal Mystery.

Press coverage, which accompanied this Apostolic Letter, provoked excitement, confusion, and questions all at once about the significance of this document. Some journalists and commentators focused only on innovation and change. A journalist friend of mine, Ann Rodgers-Melnick, confided to me that she received more letters, e-mails, telephone calls, and other inquiries from her readership than from any other church event that she covered in her entire journalistic career of some twenty-five years. The Apostolic Letter of Pope John Paul II contains within it much of the inherited reflection on the Church's spirituality and Liturgy which have already been topics of pastoral focus by prelates and scholars in the twentieth century.

The most salient feature of this letter is a renewed emphasis upon the treasures of the Bible and the importance of biblical studies. The Pontiff is developing here a theology of the Rosary, while at the same time he suggests his own personal method for the recitation of the Rosary. The addition of five new mysteries, the Luminous Mysteries of the Rosary, is intended to clarify his desire, as well as that of the Second Vatican Council, that the world recognize that the "Call to Holiness" is for everybody.

Pope John Paul II ascended the chair of Peter in 1978. He brought with him remarkable gifts of scholarship, sensitivity, linguistic talent, and a dynamic energy which by the grace of God has surpassed all attempts to thwart his effectiveness. Most of all, he is a genuinely pious individual whose consecration to the work of God has been evident in the twentieth century and beyond. I have always been taken with the Pope's love of literature and the sense of fulfillment which he derives from the use of his own pen. I have no doubt that the text of *Rosarium Virginis Mariae* flows from his mind *and his heart.*

Jerome M. Vereb, C.P.
Monastery of Saints John and Paul
Rome, Italy
November 1, 2002
Feast of All Saints

Part I

Toward a Theology
and History of the Rosary

Pope John Paul II and
His Predecessor, Pope Paul VI

A s in other aspects of his pontificate, the doctrine of Pope John Paul II furthers the teaching of his penultimate predecessor, Pope Paul VI. The first and clearest example of this deliberate magisterial pattern can be dated to the Pontiff's discourse on Evangelization at the Puebla Conference of 1979. There he addressed the entire college of Latin American Bishops gathered together in Mexico; on that important occasion, when he accepted that hierarchy's invitation, which had first been extended to Pope Paul VI and then to Pope John Paul I, for clarification regarding the meaning of the Church within a period of social and cultural upheaval there, he recalled and affirmed Paul VI's own words, already written in 1975:

"The Church is deeply aware of her duty to preach salvation to all. Knowing that the Gospel message is not reserved to a small group of the initiated, the privileged, or the elect, but is destined for everyone, she shares Christ's anguish at the sight of the wandering and exhausted crowds, like 'sheep without a shepherd,' and she often repeats His words: 'I feel sorry for all these people' " (Evangelii Nuntiandi, no. 57).

This was the premise, really, of the first phase of his pontificate. The Mystery of the Church allows for no oligarchy, no establishment, no elite. Christ is the center of all. Christ is the possession of all. The ground at the foot of the Cross is level. In this and in the other aspects of the life and ministry of the Church, he has followed the path outlined by Pope Paul VI, who was, after all, one of the two Popes of the Vatican Council.

Pope Paul VI treated the subject of the Rosary in an Apostolic Exhortation of February 2, 1974. The groundbreaking document, known as *Marialis Cultus* ("Devotion to Mary"), proved helpful in ecumenical dialogues following the Second Vatican Council. In particular, it underscored the evangelical basis of this devotion: "Thus, for instance, the Gospel inspiration of the Rosary has appeared more clearly; the Rosary draws from the Gospel the presentation of the Mysteries and its main formulas" (no. 44). Pope Paul VI emphasized that point yet again when he wrote: "As a Gospel prayer, centered on the Mystery of the redemptive Incarnation, the Rosary is therefore a prayer with a *clearly Christological orientation*" (no. 46; *emphasis, mine*). *Rosarium Virginis Mariae* picks up the theme of the primacy of Christ as the focus of all Rosary meditation.

Pope John Paul II has once again deepened and explicated the words of his predecessor. This is an important occasion, for the Pope allows himself on the occasion of his Silver Jubilee Year to display an intimate spiritual theme of his personal life: "It [the Rosary] is an echo of the prayer of Mary, her perennial *Magnificat,* for the work of the redemptive Incarnation which began in her virginal womb. With the Rosary, the Christian people *sits at the School of Mary* and is led to contemplate the beauty on the face

of Christ and to experience the depths of His love"
(*RVM*, no. 1).

These words are much more autobiographical than
they first appear in what is certainly a formal Vatican
document. This Pontiff has never hesitated to invoke an
autobiographical memory in his encyclicals and discourses, bearing in mind that as the Successor of Peter
he is a *witness (martyrion)* in the authentic sense of
"a witness before the court," whose testimony is recognized because he has been a part of the matter in question. The details of the Pontiff's youth are reflected in
the authenticity of his teaching and of his witness.

The Influence of a Neighbor

THEREFORE, in the years of the Second World War,
when most of the parish priests had been shipped
from Krakow to Dachau, the young Karol Wojtyla, then
known to his friends as "Lolek," came into the circle of
a lay mystic who lived just across the square from his
father's apartment. Lolek had already begun his philo-
sophical and literary studies at the Jagiellonian
University in Krakow in 1938. By the time Poland was
invaded on September 1, 1939, Lolek had already composed his first book of poetry, a work which indicated
his personal inclination toward the world of Christian
spirituality and mysticism. By late November 1939, the
university professors were arrested and deported to
Saxonhausen Concentration Camp, leaving the young
Wojtyla, among others, to find whatever instruction he
could in the areas of Polish art and literature, Western
philosophy, and, of course, spirituality.

In February 1940, through friends, Lolek came under the influence of his neighbor, Jan Tyranowski. Tyranowski was then forty years old, and was trained to be a business accountant, but he found the demands for precision too much for his delicate and sensitive personality. He therefore worked as a tailor, scarcely leaving his apartment, which was overcrowded with books and manuscripts. Tyranowski himself spent several hours a day in meditation and set down his colloquies in a diary in a methodical fashion, and in a fine, almost lace-like, script which revealed his very sensitive personality.

Tyranowski had first been influenced by a sermon heard in the Salesian parish church about the Polish Jesuit Scholastic, St. Stanislaus Kostka. The preacher's infinitive phrase which stuck with him was: "It is not difficult *to be a Saint.*" This experience ultimately led him to study the doctrine of the Carmelite Mystic, St. John of the Cross. Through personal study and Carmelite spiritual directors, Tyranowski was led first to a process of discernment, and then to embrace an other-worldly life. He thought it was possible to taste God through the use of the human imagination in order to experience that joy and serenity which comes from "the practice of the presence of God."

Not content to lead a hermit's life and observing the possibilities of moral decay among young men now deprived by war of clergy, teachers, and even their own fathers, Jan Tyranowski organized the youth into an organization known as "The Living

Rosary." Naturally, each fifteen-member cell comprised a fellowship, with each individual representing every decade of the Rosary. The Rosary itself stood as a symbol of a deeper type of prayer in which, as Karol Wojtyla would later recall, his style of life at that time "proved that one could not only inquire about God but also live with God." The organization prayed the Rosary, lived the Rosary, and taught the richness of the Rosary through a quartet of four mentors, of whom Lolek was one.

As time passed and the post-war era could realistically be hoped for, the members of The Living Rosary groups (by now there were several) dreamed of reestablishing "The Living Rosary" into a method of Catholic Action which carried the graces of the altar into the affairs of the marketplace to present a viable lay spirituality. All in all, their conversations and plans were not that different from the spirituality of all the Christian Churches of the East, where the moral life is synthesized by the phrase: "Living the Liturgy beyond the Liturgy."

It was during this period that Wojtyla's father died suddenly. Karol came home from study to discover the cold body in a lonely apartment. Not only was Lolek now an orphan, but he was literally without a family. Tyranowski, who was sometimes termed to be odd, presented through solitude a unique kind of spiritual maturity in what he had to offer, a holiness that was at once creative, poetic, bold, and zealous. Each time the young Wojtyla picked up his beads, he was reminded of his personal call to mysticism in this otherwise chaotic world. The recurring theme of the mystery of the Rosary, which is inherent in its inspiration and its structure, is that it represents a communion *(koinonia)* of shared "presence." The Marian prayer, *Ave Maria,* is the salutation which, in language, introduced the Incarnation of the Son of God within the human family.

Tyranowski's tutelage through St. John of the Cross, including the Carmelite classics *The Ascent of Mount Carmel, The Dark Night of the Soul, The Spiritual Canticle,* and *The Living Flame of Love,* led Lolek to a unique point of grace. He desired consecration to God. Externally, his life was one of destitution and disorientation by the affairs of war. He was almost arrested in the last roundup of Krakow's youth. Because of Tyranowski, he learned abandonment to the Will of God, and the peace of appreciating God's love for him. It was at this point that the Prince Bishop of Krakow, Cardinal Adam Sapieha, led him to the episcopal residence, educated him, and finally ordained him.

Pope John Paul II wrote of those days in his memoir, *Gift and Mystery,* which he composed for the Golden Anniversary of his priestly ordination:

> In the parish, there was one person who stood out from the others: I am speaking of *Jan Tyranowski.* By profession he was a clerk, although he had chosen to work in his father's tailor shop. He said that working as a tailor made it easier for him to develop his interior life. He was a man of especially deep spirituality. . . .

When I was in Krakow, in Debniki, I joined the "Living Rosary" group in the Salesian parish. There was a special devotion there to Mary, Help of Christians. In Debniki, at the time when my priestly vocation was developing, under the influence, as I mentioned, of Jan Tyranowski, a change took place in my understanding of devotion to the Mother of God. I was already convinced that *Mary leads us to Christ,* but at that time I began to realize also that *Christ leads us to His Mother.* At one point, I began to question my devotion to Mary, believing that, if it became too great, it might end up compromising the supremacy of the worship owed to Christ . . . (*Gift and Mystery,* pp. 23, 28).

Through the discovery of the wisdom of St. Louis Marie Grignon de Montfort in *True Devotion to the Blessed Virgin Mary,* the young Wojtyla found that Mariological thought is rooted in the *Mystery of the Trinity* and in the truth of the Incarnation of the Word of God. Furthermore, the culture of the Catholic Church reminds herself of these truths through many pious practices, including the blessing of food at mealtime, morning and evening prayers, and the daily recitation of the Angelus as well as the private and communal recitation of the Rosary. In order to experience the presence of God by the continued recollection of the ongoingness of Jesus' Incarnation, Wojtyla saw himself as a student in the School of Mary. As Pope, John Paul II adopted as his episcopal motto, *Totus Tuus ego sum et omnia mea Tua sunt* ("I am completely yours and everything I am and have is yours").

As the designer of his *stema*, or coat of arms, Archbishop Bruno Heim, then Apostolic Delegate to Great Britain, made use of an oversized "M" with an odd-shaped cross which, in the history of heraldry, has since become known as the "John Paul II Cross." The Pope's Latin motto was then reduced simply to *Totus Tuus*. From the very inception of his pontificate, Lolek, now Pope John Paul II, stated frankly: "The Rosary is my favorite prayer. A marvelous prayer! Marvelous in its simplicity and its depth."

Pope Paul VI Sets the Stage

THE presentation by Pope John Paul II of a new set of *Mysteries of the Rosary* makes great sense when seen against the insights of the Second Vatican Council and, indeed, of the fact of the Council itself. Six months before he was elected as Pope, Paul VI, then Cardinal Giovanni Battista Montini, addressed the young clergy of his diocese of Milan. The Council was still very much underway but was now in recess. The Pontiff who summoned the Council, Pope John XXIII, was already known to be ill. Cardinal Montini promised the Council's continuity due to the dynamic of the Holy Spirit.

Montini showed his hope: "At the Council, the Church is looking for itself. It is trying, with great trust and with a great effort, to define itself more precisely, and to understand what it is. After twenty centuries of history, the Church is submerged by profane civilization and absent from the contemporary world. It is therefore experiencing the need to be recollected and to purify and recover itself so as to be able to set off on its own path again with great energy."

That sentence is as true today as it was in January 1963. This clearly enunciated motive of the Council and of the Church is equally true of every Christian. As the Church was and is weighed down under so much baggage from the Ages, so too, it can be said of the adult Christian that he or she has lost the way or wandered into some dark cave. The Fathers in the Council were obviously aware of the need to re-present the Mystery of the Church as the Mystery of Christ, and they did so according to the language of St. John the Evangelist: "What has come into being in Him was life, and the life was the light *(phos)* of all people" (Jn 1:4). The Dogmatic Constitution, therefore, was called *Lumen Gentium,* "the Light of the Peoples."

Within his pontificate, it makes perfect sense, therefore, for this Pope, who was himself a Council Father, to include in the devotions of all the faithful a set of Mysteries which not only clarifies but continues the aim of the Council to receive light from the Gospel.

The Devotion of the Rosary

MANY Saints of the Church are identified with the devotion of the Rosary. For centuries now many members of Religious Orders and Congregations have also worn the Rosary as part of their religious habit. My own Religious Community, the Passionists, adopted the Rosary around 1815 as a mark of thanksgiving to Mary for the reconstitution of the Congregation after the wars of Napoleon and his secular suppression. Over time, various Passionist Generals referred to the prayer of the Rosary and the display of the Rosary as an indication that this Religious Institute, founded by St. Paul of the Cross (1693–1775), was both a memorial of the Passion and a Marian-inspired religious family.

In the late nineteenth century, Charles Martial Cardinal Lavigerie, Archbishop of Carthage and Algiers, designed the habit of his Religious Communities—the Missionaries of Africa—more commonly known since their inception in the Victorian Age as the White Fathers and White Sisters of Africa, with the Rosary worn in several strands around the neck. Most Religious Communities which displayed the Rosary as part of the habit did so by wearing the Rosary from the cincture or belt on the left side. The Redemptorists wore the Rosary as a large "M" in the front of the habit!

The tradition of displaying the Rosary on one's person derives from the Dominican tradition which enunciates the principle *Lex orandi, Lex credendi* ("The law of the prayer is the law of the believer"), linking the devotional life with the promulgation of Christian doctrine and the encouragement of the cardinal virtue of faith and its content. Through this practice, the Rosary contains an invaluable lesson: "Inner serenity is found in knowing that one believes and what one believes." In the words of Pope Paul VI: "Thus, for instance, the Gospel inspiration of the

Rosary has appeared more clearly: the Rosary draws from the Gospel the presentation of the Mysteries and its main formulas" (*Marialis Cultus,* no. 44).

The Dominican Tradition of the Rosary

CERTAINLY, the devotion of the Rosary is primarily and intimately associated with the Dominican Family of friars, nuns, and followers of the Dominican Third Order. The founder of this important Religious Family in the Church is St. Dominic de Guzman (1170-1221). Born in Old Castile, Dominic turned aside from family plans that he should enter the military and be dubbed a knight. In fact, though, two of his brothers were already priests. It was said of him that his intellectual brilliance made him a natural candidate for a court of law or for the pulpit. He chose the latter.

Trained at the ancient University of Palencia, at a time when the universities of Europe were just coming into their own as forces in society, Dominic grew to appreciate the importance of combining dogma, rhetoric, and logic. The evidence indicates that he spent much time studying the sacred texts of the Bible. He was ordained a priest for the Augustinian Canons at Osma, on the Iberian peninsula. At a very early age, he was elected prior of the community, as much for his humility and personal piety as for his intellect and oratorical skills.

In 1203, the Bishop of Osma broke Dominic's cloistered existence to invite his companionship on a diplomatic mission from the Pope to "the Marches" of France. Many of the records of this time are fragmented. What is known is that "the Marches" included territories from Denmark through France. At the same time, the Cistercian Order was founded and established by Saints Alberic, Robert of Molesmes, and Stephen Harding, as well as the great St. Bernard of Clairvaux, to be completely contemplative. "The love of learning and the desire for God," however, pressed them often into service in a manner similar to Dominic and his bishop out of obedience to the Pope.

While Rome termed this public commitment to teaching, preaching, and debate a matter of "diplomacy," all of these individuals were in fact missionaries to an unbending brand of Christianity known as Albigensianism. This movement, which affected clergy, monks, and laity, was viewed as a sect fraught with heresy that allowed little space for the love of God. Fear was the motive of their religious discipline. Along with the others, Dominic found it necessary to explain orthodox Christianity in terms of language and logic which was clear, precise, and well-premised. His skills, his charm, and his reputation for holiness attracted other clergy as followers from at least sixteen countries.

As he crossed Europe, Dominic organized a style of life for them, and he sought permission from Pope Innocent III (1198-1216) and Pope Honorius III (1226-1227) to establish them as the Order of Preachers, otherwise known today as the Dominicans. Dominic based the pattern of Dominican life on the rule of St. Augustine, and he is the first religious founder to declare that his rule did not bind under pain of sin, thus dispelling the patterns of scrupulosity which were at the heart of the Albigensian-type piety. When the opportunity arose, Dominic established the first community of Dominican Nuns at Prouille, France.

In that same city, Prouille, Dominic is said to have experienced an apparition of the Blessed Virgin Mary. Dominic was both distraught and depressed because his own preaching and that of his companions had found such little success against the intransigence of the Albigensians. Sometime in 1208, Dominic brought his frustrations to the throne of Mary, the Mother of God, through prayer. In the course of this religious experience, he begged for an intervention of mercy since the logic of his adversaries was unbending and their attitude too harsh to penetrate. Suddenly Dominic was confronted with an image of Mary. Clearly he heard her words:

"Do not be surprised that you have reaped such little fruit through your own efforts. You have spent yourself on virtually barren soil which has not yet been watered with the residue of God's grace. When God planned to renew the face of the earth [through the birth of Jesus], *He began by sending down upon it the rich, warm rain of the Angelic Salutation. Therefore, preach my psalter composed of one hundred and fifty Angelic Salutations and fifteen Our Fathers and you will obtain an abundant harvest."*

From 1208, Dominic's work of preaching, teaching, and pastoral activity was accompanied by the introduction to the devotion of the Rosary. In particular, he placed emphasis on the Joyful Mysteries of the Rosary, i.e., the Annunciation to Mary by the Angel

Gabriel, the Visitation of Mary to her cousin Elizabeth, the Birth of the Messiah at Bethlehem, the Presentation of the Infant Jesus in the Second Temple at Jerusalem, and the Finding of the Boy Jesus among the scribes and priests of the Levitical School on the temple precincts at Jerusalem.

Along with St. Dominic, St. Catherine of Siena (1347-1380) is popularly identified with the devotion of the Rosary, particularly through her catechizing the recitation of the Rosary as a form of exercising "the practice of the presence of God." Catherine Benincasa was a laywoman who adopted the Dominican habit and the Dominican way of life. Much of her time was spent in contemplative prayer, and history has identified her as a great mystic. Although withdrawn deep into the recesses of her family's home, paradoxically, during her rare appearances in the streets of Siena or on her own type of diplomatic missions to the Popes and crowned heads across Medieval Europe, she took time to teach God's little ones the secrets and the comforts of the Rosary. One might almost say that her memory is recalled by the acknowledged popularity of Mother Teresa of Calcutta.

Devotion to the Rosary is enshrined in the Italian Basilica of Our Lady of Pompeii, where a late Renaissance painting depicts Dominic and Catherine in ecstasy before the Madonna with the Infant Jesus on her lap. Copies of that picture have become familiar to most Catholics over the centuries, and its importance, like most Christian iconography, is found not so much in its texture or style but rather in the Christian truths which it portrays.

The Modern Culture of the Rosary

ON September 26, 1959, Blessed Pope John XXIII issued an Apostolic Letter entitled *Grata Recordatio* ("The Secret Memory") in which he reflected upon the devout recitation of the Rosary. He, too, outlined his own youthful dedication to this devotion. He recalled his youth, his election to the Papacy, and the present situation which confronted his Pontificate, "the sad tally of ruin and of harm wrought by armed conflict" (no. 17). He was, of course, referring to the time of the Second World War and the present conflict of the Cold War. This normally optimistic figure spoke of a world fraught with secularism and materialism, which sought the remedy to its problems through the principle of expediency, even to the point of nuclear annihilation. He encouraged the faithful to take their "fervent prayers to the august Virgin Mary" (no. 15).

In the first sentences of his communiqué, Pope John XXIII defined the Rosary: "The Rosary, as is known to all, is in fact a very excellent means of prayer and meditation in the form of a mystical crown in which the prayers 'Our Father,' 'Hail Mary' and 'Glory Be to the Father' are intertwined with meditation upon the greatest Mysteries of our faith, and which presents to the mind, like many pictures, the drama of the Incarnation of our Lord and the Redemption" (no. 4). The Pontiff went on to relay that from "the sweet memory of our young years" until the present time, he recited the Rosary daily and often (no. 5).

This fact is true. A recent visit to the late Pontiff's former secretary, Archbishop Loris Capovilla, at Casa Roncalli revealed that there were three continuous pillars to Pope John XXIII's spirituality: (1) meditation on the Crucifix and the Passion of Jesus (one of his favorite books was *The Folly of the Cross,* by Raoul Plus, S.J.), (2) the daily *Ignatian examen,* in which he chose "humility" as the core grace of his reflection and petition, and (3) the daily recitation of the Rosary, both privately in the course of the day and later as Bishop, Cardinal Patriarch, and Pope after supper with all the members of his household.

The content of Pope John XXIII's Apostolic Letter is not foreign to me personally. I, like many others, grew up in a "culture of the Rosary." From this vantage point, it is not hard to appreciate that my parents and my parish priests used the instrument of the Rosary to teach me about God. I clearly remember my mother teaching me the succession of Our Fathers and Hail Marys at a time before I even started school. It was customary for my father to come home early from work in later years and to say, "Get your homework done early, son; we have to go to the funeral home to say the Rosary." Sometimes we would take two or three streetcars to arrive on time to recite the Rosary at 9:00 P.M. to conclude the Wake Service of a dear friend or family member.

I remember that, despite the fatigue of a day's work, both my parents and I would often brave even snowy weather to participate in the communal recitation of the Rosary as an expression of our faith in the life of the Resurrection, as a comfort for the bereaved, and as a way of accompanying the soul of the departed through heaven's gates. My parents' faith was simple, strong, and consistent. Needless to say, we also recited the Rosary at home, gathered around the radio, while Monsignor Paul Bassompierre led the Rosary across the airwaves.

The public recitation of the Rosary was a particular Apostolate in the Diocese of Pittsburgh of Monsignor Bassompierre, who was noted for his heroic work among the poor. My parish priests also were dedicated to the Rosary. I can remember that during my high school years Father Thomas Gearing, pastor of the parish of St. Canice, my home parish, removed his vestments after the Mass he celebrated and made his Eucharistic thanksgiving at the Pietà statue in our wide and poorly appointed church. So, too, did the priest who was my pastor at the time of my ordination to the priesthood, Monsignor Joseph Findlan. Although retired for almost twenty years, Monsignor Findlan, now over ninety, maintains this custom as he does daily supply work in neighboring parishes or convents.

Most heroic of all in this regard, however, was the pastor of my youth, Father John C. Fallon. This hearty cleric was born in Ireland at the end of the nineteenth century and he served as pastor of our territorial parish, St. Canice, in the Knoxville section of Pittsburgh. His memory is still cherished as people recall that he never owned a car or rode the trolley, and he rarely asked someone to drive him. He walked everywhere. The Rosary was his constant companion. At suppertime, he would walk into neighborhood homes, pray the Rosary with the family, and then promptly leave, refusing all offers for dinner. I clearly remember him breaking up a baseball game or gathering "the kids" with their roller skates so that the youth of the parish not only knew how to say the Rosary but also appreciated its value.

Other examples include meetings of the Christian Mothers Guild, who gathered to pray their sons safely through the Korean War, and Monsignor Paul Lackner, a son of my parish, who led literally hundreds of Catholic men in procession through the downtown streets of Pittsburgh reciting the Rosary in honor of the Holy Name and condemning, at the same time, the distribution of pornographic literature and the widespread use of profane language.

My entrance into the Passionists in 1965 uncovered another devotion of the Rosary. For one thing, the founder of the Passionists, St. Paul of the Cross, had enrolled all his present and future novices in the Confraternity of the Rosary so that, besides the community recitation, the novices walked in procession in late afternoon to say the Rosary a second time. In my Passionist student life, it was customary to celebrate the Feast of Our Lady of the Rosary publicly, especially so at the monastery in Jamaica, New York, where large groups of Catholic men joined the religious community in a night-time public demonstration through the streets of Queens.

All of these events are now long past, but they bespeak the persistence of a culture which taught the truths of the Christian faith by both personal and public example. This is the "Culture of the Rosary," alluded to by Pope John XXIII in his 1959 *Grata Recordatio.*

Although Pope Paul VI alluded to the Rosary in his Apostolic Letter, *Marialis Cultus,* of 1974, this new Apostolic Letter, *Rosarium Virginis Mariae,* is the direct successor to the one written by Pope John XXIII in 1959, and it bears some comparison. Also written in an autobiographical style, it identifies a special and powerful role of Mary in the Economy of Salvation. It likewise makes reference to the power of "Luminous prayer" in an age fraught with shadows and specters.

As has been stated, Pope John Paul II declared that the Rosary was his favorite prayer. That admission was associated with the Pope's pilgrimage of thanksgiving to the mountain-high Marian Shrine at Mentorella, Italy, after his election as Pope. Now, having just returned from Poland, Pope John Paul II states that his recent visit to the Marian Shrine of Kalwaria in Poland in 2002 had an effect on the composition of this present Apostolic Letter. *Rosarium Virginis Mariae* is more lengthy than the letter of Pope John XXIII; likewise it is rich in content, and, in view of the insights of the Second Vatican Council, it sheds new light on a traditional form of popular spirituality.

Neither imperious, nor confrontational, nor disciplinary, *Rosarium Virginis Mariae* is but one more example of the Pope's commitment to the apostolate of catechesis. A careful study indicates that the following points are outstanding: (1) the Mystery of Christ, (2) the School of Mary, (3) the importance of the *Ave Maria*, (4) the structure of the Rosary, and (5) the necessity of silence.

The Mystery of Christ

AS prelate and pedagogue, Karol Wojtyla had ample opportunity to imbibe the theological developments of the twentieth century. Principally in the Christian countries of northern Europe, amidst the rise of detached attitudes toward religion, a new trend of Catholic thought was born. Known as the kerygmatic school of catechesis, it focused attention on the significance of the historical Jesus in the Christ-event. Principal proponents were Pius Parsh for Liturgy, Romano Guardini for both devotion and systematics, and Karl Adam for theology. The writings of Adam are not to be underplayed at all. It was Adam who clearly explained the reasons for the Christian's communion with God and with one another in Christ. He did so by the very title of his seminal work, *Christ Our Brother.* According to him, not only is Jesus accessible because of His humanity but He also makes the Father accessible to humanity. In one place he has written, "Man belongs to God as the sheep belongs to its shepherd and master, and depends on him for his very being and his every act."

But contingency is not the only motive. Instead, according to Adam, the central theme of the Christ-event is the important place that Jesus gives to His relationship to His Heavenly Father. Like the others of this school, Adam relied heavily on the sacred texts of the Bible to illustrate his point. Because all are adopted sons of the Father, and therefore, according to the Pauline text, "all are in Christ," Adam presented that the core insight of the Christ-event is a theology of love, both given and received. "And God raised us up with Christ and seated us with Him in the heavenly realms in Christ Jesus, in order that in the coming ages, He might show the incomparable riches of His grace, expressed in His kindness to us *in Christ Jesus*" (Eph 2:6).

Therefore, as a child of his era, a student of his theological environment, and the principal interpreter of the insights of the Second Vatican Council, Pope John Paul II has placed the primacy of this and all his theological discourse on the Christological theme that he emphasized in his first encyclical, *Redemptor Hominis* ("The Redeemer of Man"), which above all other things reminded humanity that God "loved the world" (Jn 3:16). This sense of love and of the primacy of Christ motivated the encyclical which was his first formal teaching.

The third section of *Rosarium Virginis Mariae* displays Pope John Paul II's consistent thought as well as the heart of the text:

In Christ, God has truly assumed a "heart of flesh." Not only does God have a divine heart, rich in mercy and in forgiveness, but also a human heart, capable of all the stirrings of affection. If we needed evidence of this from the Gospel, we could easily find it in the touching dialogue between Christ and Peter after the Resurrection: "Simon, son of John, do you love Me?" Three times this question is put to Peter and three times he gives the reply: "Lord, You know that I love You" (Jn 21:15-17).

Over and above the specific meaning of this passage, so important for Peter's mission, none can fail to recognize the beauty of this triple repetition, in which the insistent request and the corresponding reply are expressed in terms familiar from the universal experience of human love. To understand the Rosary, one has to enter into the psychological dynamic proper to love (no. 26).

The mediation between God and the human community is the Life of Christ, Who is Son of God, Lord, High Priest, Messiah, Savior, and Brother. The Pope himself recalls this point by making reference to the *Catholic Catechism* of 1992, which states that the events of Christ's life are a mediation of communion between God and humankind. The *Catholic Catechism* is a remarkable source for the Pope's meditation here, for it synthesizes Christological doctrine in light of the renewed biblically-based insights stemming from the Second Vatican Council.

The Contribution of the Second Vatican Council

THAT Council was also the product of the various schools of twentieth-century Personalist philosophy, which stated that every individual in Creation is not only *something,* but, even more importantly, *someone* —i.e., a human being, capable of giving and receiving the gracious love of God. Therefore, the *Catholic Catechism* states: "The coming of God's Son to earth is an event of *such immensity* that God willed to prepare for it over centuries. He makes *everything converge on Christ:* all the rituals and sacrifices, figures and symbols of the 'First Covenant.' He announces him through the mouths of the prophets, who succeeded one another in Israel. Moreover, He awakens in the hearts of the pagans a dim expectation of this coming" (no. 522; *emphasis, mine*).

Under the direction of Pope John Paul II and with the consensus of the Mixed Commission which compiled it, the *Catechism* goes on to explain that Christ's *whole life* is the Mystery of Redemption. It genuinely means His *whole life,* His words and deeds, His silences and sufferings, indeed, His manner of being and speaking. All of this is the Expression of the Father. The Father has said: "This is My Son, My Chosen; listen to Him" (Mk 9:7). For His part, Jesus has said: "Whoever has seen Me has seen the Father" (Jn 14:9). The events of the life of Christ invite communion with God and communion with one another, in what Christian theology of the East calls "the family of love."

The Sacramental life of the Church, i.e., the Sacraments, the Worship, the Proclamation of Sacred Scripture, the Preaching, draws an assembly to experience the presence of God through many modes—(1) the community, (2) the poverty of the worshipers, (3) the Word of God itself, (4) the ministry of the Ordained, and, above all, (5) the Eucharist. Since, in this setting, all are invited to identify themselves with the Royal

Priesthood of Christ, all are participants in this celebration of the Liturgy and share in the dignity of Jesus the Royal High Priest, especially at the time of worship. Given this truth, the Christian pattern of moral philosophy substantiates the image of "engagement," i.e., a marketplace ethics, where the Liturgy is celebrated beyond the Liturgy, especially in daily work and living.

Herein, both sacramentally and morally, Jesus is "our model" (*Catholic Catechism*, no. 520). The actions of Jesus, whether by deeds or words, invite discipleship. Those who witness Jesus' miracles and parables are indeed disciples who have been invited to follow Him. There are real human emotions displayed in Jesus' Public Life. He attends festivities. He weeps at the death of His friend. He is rudely confronted by challengers to His teaching, but He gives us an example for imitation. We see Him in poverty, at prayer, in privation, and under persecution. Curiously, as the Rosary became popular in the Middle Ages and spread across Europe, and eventually to the Americas, to Asia and to Africa, it was paralleled in popularity by the little book of Thomas a Kempis, *The Imitation of Christ*. The doctrine of Christ, our Model, provides the corollary of morality, "to be and to do as Jesus did." This is the imitation of Christ. It is also known as the School of Jesus.

Christ: The Center of the Rosary

THE School of Jesus is essentially a drama in which there are two principal characters—the teacher (rabbi) and the student or the disciple. Discipleship of

Jesus is, realistically and within the tradition of Christian spirituality, pivoted upon the actual discipleship of those who followed Jesus, observed Him, and heard His words in the first century. These are recorded in Scripture. Not to pay attention to them leads to mere fantasy or vulnerability to the pressures of changing times. Trends come and go, as do cultures. The School of Jesus stands apart from civilizations; it is never intended to bolster up the establishment.

The School of Jesus focuses upon the person of Jesus, and is the ultimate expression of the doctrine that the Incarnation is the high point of God's Self-Revelation. The biblical scholar James G. Dunn has said: "All other claims to understand God and the will of God have to be read in its light. As far as Christians are concerned, all other such claims have to be brought to the touchstone of the historical Revelation of God in Christ." To use ordinary jargon: "Jesus knows the way, goes the way, shows the way." The first Christians at Jerusalem were called, in fact, "the people of the Way."

As to the content of Jesus' teaching, first and foremost, according to the commentary of the great exegete Joachim Jeremias, is Jesus' passionate devotion to His Heavenly Father. The evangelists are unanimous in expressing that this is the core of His teaching. It is innovative in Hebrew theology and spirituality. Jesus' desire to enact the unconditional surrender of His whole being to the Divine Will is not based on a sense of obligation to extraneous law. For Jesus, this Father was not the pale and distant deity of contemporary Hellenistic philosophy, or of that late Jewish theology which was so much influenced by it. He was no remote God, sitting enthroned above the clouds, in solitary silence and maintaining contact with men only through angelic hosts.

He is the Living God of Revelation. Here the Master's teaching is linked up with the pure preaching of the prophets, wherein God was set forth emphatically as the most living and personal presence and power. The greatest example of this truth is the moment when Jesus took the little child and set him in the middle of the listeners and the apostles, and told them that this was the symbol of the Kingdom of God. One had to become like this in order to get into the Kingdom of Heaven. The richness of this gesture becomes clear when one recalls that Christ Himself so configured His ministry as to express that He was the child of His own Father. This in fact is the meaning of the place of the incident of the Finding of the Boy Jesus in the Temple in the Lucan Nativity account.

Modern biblical scholars, such as Raymond E. Brown, have made careful study of the structure of the Infancy Account determining that the actual narrative of the coming of the Messiah ended with chapter two, verse 40. The remaining passages in chapter two, verses 41-51, which deal with the disappearance of Jesus from the procession returning home to Nazareth from the Passover celebration at the Temple in Jerusalem, represent an interest in the Hidden Life of Jesus. Evidence of such interest is found in the Apocryphal gospels, which were prevalent in the primitive Christian communities in Egypt in the second century.

In this incident, scholars find evidence that Jesus sitting among the teachers is a teacher Himself. His Mother became His first student. "Why were you searching for Me?" He asked. "Didn't you know I had to be in My Father's house?"... Then He went down to Nazareth with them and was obedient to them. But His Mother treasured all these things in her heart. Then Jesus grew with wisdom and stature, and in favor with God and men" (Lk 2:49-52).

The obvious point is the priority given to His Divine Sonship and that of the adopted sons and daughters of God the Father, and, therefore, brothers and sisters in Christ. As the doctrine of the Public Ministry of Jesus will reveal later in the Gospels, the teaching about one's attachment to Christ is paradoxical, a seeming contradiction. For in a later passage, Jesus contrasts "My Father" with "your father." Then, despite the fact that He was endowed with wisdom, knowledge, and grace, He returned from the house of His Father to Nazareth to absorb training and growth under Joseph, whom the world saw as His father. This is the first lesson of Jesus' School.

The School of Jesus is apocalyptic, i.e., it is about the disclosure of the secrets of the Kingdom of Heaven, and is grounded in the hope that eventually all things will be revealed. "My meat and drink is to do the will of Him that sent Me" (Jn 4:34).

The School of Jesus

THEREFORE, Pope John Paul II has explained his reasons for adding a new set of Mysteries to broaden the understanding of the importance of the School of Jesus. Since it is the Pontiff's belief that the Rosary is the School of Jesus, it must be viewed to become more fully a compendium of the Gospel. It is appropriate to add to the Rosary so that the content of Jesus the Teacher might be appreciated and therefore enrich the individual's relationship with Christ, Who is not only our Teacher but our Brother. Therefore Pope John Paul II has, in his own words, given us this statement of purpose:

I believe, however, that to bring out fully the Christological depth of the Rosary, it would be suitable to make an addition to the traditional pattern which, while left to the freedom of individuals and communities, could broaden it to include *the Mysteries of Christ's Public Ministry between His Baptism and His Passion.* In the course of those ministries, we *contemplate important aspects of the person of Christ as the definitive revelation of God [emphasis, mine].* Declared the beloved Son of the Father at the Baptism in the Jordan, Christ is the One Who announces the coming of the Kingdom, bears witness to it in His works, and proclaims its demands. It is during the years of His Public Ministry that the *Mystery of Christ is most evidently a mystery of life:* " 'While I am in the world, I am the Light of the World' (Jn 9:5)" (*RVM,* no. 19).

On the day of the Inauguration of his Pontificate in the Square of St. Peter's Basilica, as a member of the

Secretariat for Promoting Christian Unity, I suddenly witnessed the Pope leave the area of the altar and come down to face the crowd, carrying his crozier, which is shaped in the form of a crucifix. This gesture was ecumenical in character because the Pope stood among the representatives of the various Churches and ecclesial communities who had come to join in the celebration of John Paul II's election and the inception of his Petrine ministry. By chance, I found that he came to be standing next to me, and I felt the thrill of the crowd as he spontaneously lifted his crozier and dramatically pointed to the figure of Christ on the Cross. It therefore came as no surprise to me to read in his first encyclical, *Redemptor Hominis* ("The Redeemer of Man"), which is entirely devoted to the Mystery of Christ:

> All of us who are Christ's followers must therefore meet and unite around Him. . . . We can and we must immediately reach and display to the world our unity in proclaiming the *Mystery of Christ,* in revealing the divine dimension and also the human dimension of the Redemption, and in struggling with unwearying perseverance *for the dignity that each human being has reached and can continually reach in Christ.* . . . Jesus Christ is the stable principle and fixed center of the mission that God Himself has entrusted to man" (no. 11; *emphasis, mine*).

The content of *Rosarium Virginis Mariae* is a deepening of the doctrinal importance contained in the Papal gestures and teachings since the day of Karol Wojtyla's election as Pope. Now he writes, "In the light of what has been said so far on the Mysteries of Christ, it is not difficult to go deeper into the *anthropological significance* of the Rosary which is far deeper than may appear at first sight"(*RVM*, no. 25). By the method which he proposes, and the *Luminous Mysteries of the Rosary* which he promulgates, Pope John Paul II warmly invites one and all to the life of holiness declared by the Council and the mysticism which is inherent in the teaching of Christ. To put it in simple words, to look below the surface of life, and to see what is really there, is the content of the Rosary as the School of Christ.

The School of Mary

IN the history of Christian spirituality, many great figures of the Church have indeed made reference to a school of Marian spirituality. Among them are St. Bernard of Clairvaux, St. Teresa of Avila, St. John of the Cross, St. Alphonsus Liguori, St. Margaret Mary Alacoque, St. Catherine Labouré, St. Louis Marie Grignon de Monfort, St. Gabriel Possenti of Our Lady of Sorrows, St. Padre Pio of Pietrelcina, Blessed Bartolo Longo, the Servant of God Mother Mary Potter, foundress of the Little Company of Mary, and the Irish-born Father Patrick Peyton, C.S.C., who is best known throughout the world for his proverb, *"The family that prays together stays together."* However, great emphasis must also be placed upon the teaching of St. Ignatius Loyola, who so structured the composition of the *Spiritual Exercises* that the second week of this special thirty-day prayer period is devoted to the Proclamation of the Kingdom of God by attention to Jesus' Public Ministry.

Ignatius was given neither to oversimplification nor to sterile methods of discursive prayer. He did not wish to leave the exercitant with a series of syllogisms. He dedicated the Second through the Fourth Week of the *Spiritual Exercises* to focus upon the ministry of Jesus, His victory over Satan, the "Discernment of Spirits," and the consecration of oneself to God's glory. According to one Ignatian authority, Christopher F. Mooney, S.J.: "Dependence of the soul (in these *Exercises* the grace of the Holy Spirit is absolute), the ultimate orientation of the Christian commitment to the glory of God, requires *generosity* toward God and the people of God. Each day through daily prayer and the Ignatian examen, the individual accepts the daily challenge to identify the *magis* or the *mas*, i.e., 'the more.'"

This Jesuit concept, so well outlined in the recently republished book, *Ignatius the Theologian*, by Hugo Rahner, S.J., is not reserved to any cluster of the spiritual elite. It is a commonsense epigram or phrase of the committed Christian, and is identified with "love" as the essence of Jesus' teaching. My own mother used to recall for me her own proverb. "Son," she would say, "the man who does only what he is supposed to do can never expect to do or receive anything *more*." The sentence remained a part of her personal wisdom, and, after her death, I realized that it inspired her own generous service and her special gift of transparency. In this Ignatian context, Mary holds her own proper place.

At every critical juncture of the *Exercises*, the spiritual director advises the retreatant to pray to Mary first, especially by viewing life through Mary's eyes, before taking the matter to Christ and to the Father in prayer. A colloquy of the Second Week, therefore, begins with reflection upon an incident not recorded in Sacred Scripture, i.e., the leave-taking of Jesus from Mary's home at Nazareth. One is meant to *feel* the parting of Mother and Son. Secondly, one enters into the compelling "sense of mission" which Jesus is receiving from His Father. In a follow-up meditation, Ignatius presents Jesus in the home of relatives in Galilee, where He has stopped to explain what He has to do, as a wandering Rabbi, in those uncertain times of Roman-occupied Palestine.

My reflection on the personalities of Jesus and Mary, at such a moment of exigency, comes from the thought of the historian Herbert Butterfield, who said that history is the process of reflecting upon personalities, even to the point of putting them through the mill. The very vicissitudes of such a process present a personality in "a finer texture." The Ignatian motif follows just such a process by the recall of a crucial moment which, while not recorded in the New Testament, certainly took place. It teaches us a very valuable lesson that the action of the Master is explained by the attitude and the deeds of the disciple-mother-precursor. Mary's *Fiat* ("May it thus be done") came before the

Fiat of Jesus, regarding both His public career and the prayer of Jesus in the Garden (Lk 22:42).

This is the School of Mary. It is the complete surrender to the Mystery of God by accepting the Will of God for one's life story and all its components. Without foresight into her personal future, Mary surrendered to the mystery of her vocation to be the Mother of God. Ignatius has structured the *Exercises* so that the retreatant might be drawn into the invitation of Mary's *Fiat* because *she* is the first disciple. She heard the message of the angel. She believed. Yet, at the same time, she expressed common sense and a reasonable nature. She was led to wonder, like the rest of us in the Christian dispensation, but she trusted that God would lovingly and freely operate within her life to enable the Word Incarnate to achieve ultimate victory.

Mary's place in the New Testament presents the best example of the Christian's call to participate likewise in Christ's "Cosmic Redemption" and in the *laudem gloriae Trinitatis* ("the praise of the glory of the Trinity"). At this juncture, as Jesus begins His Public Ministry, Ignatius directs a retreatant's attention to the fact that Mary, having lived so intimately the Mystery with Jesus, must now perform the hardest task of all. She must let Him go.

The life of Jesus clearly shows that God did not lightly deal with Miriam of Nazareth, i.e., Mary. Pope John Paul II was already emphatic about this in his eleventh Encyclical, *Evangelium Vitae* ("The Gospel of Life"), in 1995: "Like the Church, Mary too had to

live her motherhood amid suffering. 'This Child is set
... for a sign that is spoken against—and a sword will
pierce through your own soul also—that thoughts out
of many hearts may be revealed' (Lk 2:34-35). The
words which Simeon addresses to Mary at the very
beginning of the Savior's earthly life sum up and pre-
figure the rejection of Jesus and, with Him, of Mary,
a rejection that reached its culmination on Calvary"
(no. 103). Again, Mary was the precursor, for the
release of Jesus from her arms at Nazareth was her
moment of *kenosis*, i.e., giving generously of one's
self until there is nothing left to give.

That *kenosis* was dramatically demonstrated by
the figure of Mary in the Calvary group at the foot of
the Cross on Good Friday. From recent discoveries of
Roman history, with its cruel punishment of crucifixion, we realize now that her place there was associated with all the components of the Roman method
of crucifixion. This brutal form of execution, devised
earlier by the Syrians and carried out by the Romans
in the first century, subjected the victim to the cru-
elest kinds of pain, beginning with a brutal scourging, which was intended to create infection and in-
stant fever so that the victim was disoriented; then,
once hung up on the cross, the prisoner was even
stripped of his loincloth, while it was announced that
his name was now blotted out from the public record
and could be pronounced no more.

This is why the High Priests went to Pilate to
protest that he had written a title and placed it above
Jesus' head, when, in fact, custom dictated that from

the moment of condemnation Jesus was a non-person (Jn 19:20-21). Like the two thieves crucified with Him, Jesus was called a *momser,* i.e., one who had no mother or whose mother was a "loose" woman. This practice of shame was intended to cause the victim psychological pain as he heard his mother disgraced and degraded.

The Pope continued in *Evangelium Vitae* the message that Mary shares the gift which her Son makes of Himself *(kenosis)* (no. 103). She offers Jesus, gives Him over, and begets Him to the end, for our sake. The "yes" spoken on the day of the Annunciation reached full maturity on the "Day of the Cross," when the time came for Mary to receive and beget as her children all those who became her disciples by themselves entering the Mystery. "When Jesus saw His Mother, and the disciple whom He loved, standing near, He said to His Mother, 'Woman, behold your Son' " (Jn 19:26).

This was the thought of Ignatius of Loyola whose *Spiritual Exercises,* which are all about making hard choices, insisted that reflections and meditations commence with reference to Mary.

The harshness of Mary's life is seen in the birth of the Messiah in poverty without sanitary conditions. It is certainly found in the passage about the flight into Egypt. Mary undoubtedly experienced anxiety and distress when the boy Jesus was lost. Jesus seemingly humiliated her, not only at the incident of Cana, when He did not immediately do her bidding, but also through His seemingly sharp words regarding Mary, when told of her presence among the crowds during His evangelical journeys.

The School of Mary presents Mary's curriculum as a series of lessons in consistency, piety, fidelity, humility, fortitude, and meekness. Of course, she is also our unsurpassed model of the cardinal virtues of faith, hope, and love. Like the rest of us, she did not achieve immediate answers to her questions. She too had to stir up the kettle of language in order to come up with new words to rephrase her questions. She yet appears as a woman of faith and trust in the mightiness and the Godly consistency of the Most Blessed Trinity, in Whose presence she most certainly lived.

Marian shrines are found all over the world: in the Roman Basilica of St. Mary Major, Jasna Gòra, Ephesus, Mexico City, and of course, Fatima, to which the Pontiff has made many pilgrimages since the assassination attempt made on his life on May 13, 1981. Many have categorized Marian devotions connected with these places as merely representative of frivolity, superstition, or, at best, a carry-over from the Romantic piety of the late nineteenth century. Yet, the greatest site of pilgrimage is Lourdes where, in 1858, Mary is said to have come to St. Bernadette Soubirous, a fourteen-year-old peasant girl who suffered the stigma of poverty, asthma, and misunderstanding at the hands of family, schoolmates, and even the nuns who taught her.

On February 11 of that year, Bernadette had a religious experience which was later accepted to be an apparition of Mary. The iconography of Lourdes portrays Mary as carrying a Rosary. For a long time,

Bernadette's story was disbelieved or else portrayed as saccharine entertainment. In a discourse given in Rome in 1981, Pope John Paul II pierced the patina of this bourgeois approach. He said:

> "The story of Lourdes is a poem of Mary's motherly love, always vigilant and concerned about her children, and it also sums up the history of so much human suffering, which has become prayer, offering confident *abandonment to God's will, drawing from it comfort, serenity, meaning, and value for one's own suffering. May the Blessed Virgin, from the grotto of Massabielle [Lourdes], give to you too, as to so many sick people, today and always, a smile, an encouragement, a grace that will relieve you and comfort you on your way of suffering."*

The above-cited words express the significance of the Pope's recent identification of the Rosary with the School of Mary. Mary, too, is a participant witness *(martyrion)*. She has come to her role in Salvation History, like the rest of us, without any road-map or guide, without any script or stage direction. She, too, has had to rely on the prompting of grace and the presence of the Holy Spirit. Her charge was to accept, in hope, the uncanny events of her life and that of her Son. Ultimate meaning is found only in the *great plan of God*. Through the School of Mary, one sees that Mary herself is the precedent, the first disciple, the first human contact with God's secret plan, the first to hear the Good

News through the message of the angel, and the first to feel, through the Mystery of Christ, the action of the Holy Spirit.

The School of Mary also enunciates one capital rule of study. It is the task of each student to observe and focus upon the face of Christ, like Mary. He is the "light of the world" (Jn 8:12). That light is best seen during the years of Jesus' Public Life *when He proclaims the Gospel of the Kingdom,* the substance of His teaching. The School of Mary dares to approach Christ and to speak to Him about great secrets which arise in every human heart, i.e., the desire for meaning, the desire to have one's hopes satisfied, the desire to experience love. This last is most obvious. The normal, artistic image of Mary is that of the Madonna, which is the expression of unqualified love between mother and child.

In *Rosarium Virginis Mariae,* Pope John Paul II praised St. Ignatius Loyola for the component of discursive prayer which focuses on the importance of the imagination, which, in turn, allows each person to enter the Mystery. St. Francis of Assisi did this by his method of preaching, through which the listener was encouraged to follow the words and to imagine the scene. Influenced by Francis, Ignatius taught the method of *compositio loci*—"the mind's composition of place."

Observing Jesus, with the companionship of Mary, through the deliberate, silent, and creative use of the imagination, is at the heart of the Rosary, the School of Mary, which "corresponds *to the inner logic of the Incarnation*" (*RVM,* no. 29). God *wanted* to take on human features. He did so through His bodily reality, which, in turn, led to His Sacramental reality. In the Sacrament of the Church, the Seven Sacraments of Grace, and the Sacrament of Scripture, we are led to that greatest of all gifts, the experience of the presence of God "in my heart, by grace."

The *Ave Maria* Prayer

IN the Apostolic Letter, *Rosarium Virginis Mariae,* Pope John Paul II squarely faced the issue that many find the recitation of the Rosary difficult. Those who are uncomfortable with the prayer of the Rosary are certainly in good company. Many Saints have felt the same way. St. Teresa of Avila, for example, freely admitted failure with her attempts to say the Rosary. Paradoxically, Teresa, who was recognized as a great Carmelite mystic and a Doctor of the Church, was akin to Ignatius of Loyola as his contemporary in both time and thought. She too promoted devotion to Mary, and defined prayer as "conversation with Christ" in His Mysteries.

Unfortunately, at the dawn of the new millennium, many remain ignorant of the potential of the Rosary or simply devalue it. Twenty years in Rome have given me ample opportunity to observe parents and grandparents in search of some appropriate souvenir for their children or grandchildren. Usually they would settle upon Rosary beads which they would have blessed by the Pope in the course of his Wednesday General Audience. This gesture was done in good faith, certainly. These Rosaries were meant to represent all that Christian Rome stood for—the catacombs, the ancient churches and basilicas, the shrines of Saints Peter and Paul, the tombs of recently beatified or canonized Saints, and the person of the Pope himself.

However, once home, the Rosary had two possible futures, especially if the child or individual was ignorant of either its purpose or its methodology. It might be interpreted as a piece of jewelry or a plaything, and thus be easily broken, or else it might find itself in some drawer. Some people hang a Rosary in their house or car as a mark of superstition. Unless accompanied by instruction, which in fact should be somewhat detailed, the gift of the Rosary is at risk of "being wrongly devalued, and therefore no longer taught to the younger generation" (*RVM*, no. 4). In the Apostolic Letter, the Pope addresses this issue by explaining the Mystery of the Rosary. He says that the key to understanding the Rosary is to see it first as a school of prayer and a path of contemplation (*RVM*, no. 5).

John Paul goes on to state: "The Rosary, precisely because it starts with Mary's own experience, is an *"exquisitely contemplative prayer"* (*RVM*, no. 12). This, of course, follows the Lucan description of Mary's "wonder": "And Mary kept all these things, pondering them in her heart. . . . The Child's father and mother marveled at what was said about Him" (Lk 2:33).

The Pontiff further develops his theme: "The Contemplation of Christ has an *incomparable model* in Mary. In a unique way the face of the Son belongs to Mary. It was in her womb that Christ was formed, receiving from her a human resemblance which points to an even greater spiritual closeness. No one has ever devoted himself to the contemplation of the face of Christ as faithfully as Mary. The eyes of her heart already turned to Him at the Annunciation, when she conceived Him by the power of the Holy Spirit" (*RVM*, no.10).

As a prelude to his teaching about the contemplative possibilities of the Rosary, the Pope indicates that the Rosary is the prayer of the Christian to Christ through Mary: "The Rosary belongs among the finest and most praiseworthy traditions of Christian contemplation. Developed in the West, it is a typically meditative prayer, corresponding in some way to the 'prayer of the heart' or 'Jesus prayer' which took root in the soil of the Christian East" (*RVM*, no. 5).

This last reference, so popular among Eastern monastics, pilgrims, and, in the nineteenth century, even the intelligentsia of Russia and Constantinople, is called *Hesychistic* prayer. In 1961, this prayer method was made popular again through the publication of J.D. Salinger's *Franny and Zooey*. He based his two short stories upon the popular Orthodox pamphlet, *The Way of the Pilgrim*, which recalls the uniqueness of Orthodox piety.

This Patristic tradition treasures the concept of *onomatōlatreia*, which deems the sacred name of Jesus as the vessel of the presence of the Divinity of Christ. It is the most consistent and one of the most interesting aspects of Eastern mysticism. It invites the mind to go back into the heart. This practice is called *omphalōscōpia*, a method, differing from individual to individual, which, at first, places the body at rest and regulates the breathing. Here one finds a state of prayer, i.e., a contemplative discipline with rules of asceticism, in which the soul experiences, through repetition and a bodily quiet, a sense of serenity, which is akin to feeling the divine light.

The Jesus Prayer, as taught by the *Philocalia,* an ancient compendium of Eastern mysticism dating back to the late Patristic age, is most popularly exercised by saying: *"Lord Jesus Christ, Son of David, have mercy on me a sinner."* The prayer is recited according to the patterns of tonic rhythm. Therefore, the prayer would read: *Lord/Jesus Christ/Son of David/have mercy/on me a sinner.* Notice that this formula first invokes the name of Jesus. Further, the prayer has always been viewed in the Eastern Churches as a deliberate and formal expression, through repetitive prayer, which, in itself, is the popular response to the mandate of St. Paul: "Pray always" (1 Thes 5:16).

The repetition of these words remains constant throughout the day until the focused attention actually joins one's breathing pattern. There is evidence that Eastern Christians have traditionally held such a manner of prayer as the practice of the presence of God to be so effective because of its consistency.

Such repetitive prayer is indeed very ancient and has been found in the evidence of cultic practices, as well as in religious traditions other than Christian. Liturgically or interiorly, the Orthodox Jew recites over and over again: *"Shema, O Ysrael, Addonai elle-henu Ahod"* ("Hear, O Israel, the Lord your God is One"). Members of the Islamic faith are accustomed to repeating *"Aijin Allah, Allah aijin Allah"* ("There is one God and that God is Allah"). Both invocations arise from the Patriarchal Tradition, including Abraham, Joseph, and Moses. Both prayers are similar in that they proclaim God's majesty, the mighty *Oneness* of God. Among the Jewish and Muslim faithful, both formulae produce sentiments of veneration, sober repentance, and the cry for mercy. The practice of such prayer, so common in Islamic and Jewish communities alike, pivots upon training oneself to actually hear the words not only with ears open to external sound but also with the intuition of the heart.

In the Christian tradition, the *Ave Maria* became the anthropological successor in this pattern of repetitive prayer. The *Ave Maria* is thought to have been devised in the fifth century C.E., and coupled with the Angelic Salutation and the veneration of Mary as the *Theotokos* (the God-bearer) by the decree of the Council of Ephesus in 431. This prayer was first structured as a *pastiche,* i.e., an art form structured from language or symbols of other places. It was composed of non-continuous sentences from the Infancy Narrative of St. Luke's Gospel (1:28, 42). The name "Jesus" was appended at the end of the recitation. The *Ave Maria,* too, originally recited in Latin, follows the musical patterns of tonic rhythm. The arrangement of tonal vowels and syllables is intended to climax with the pronunciation of the name of Jesus.

An appreciation of this prayer, as Mary's memory, is best seen in its poetic arrangement through the Latin formula.

Ave Maria
gratia plena
Dominus tecum
benedicta tu in mulieribus
et benedictus/fructus/ventris tui
Jesus!

First and foremost, it must be pointed out that, unlike the Islamic and Hebrew formulae cited above, or even the *Hesychistic* prayer of the East, this text does not focus on God's sovereignty, but rather on God's action and presence among men and women in human history. History shows that this ecclesiastical formula has a devotional expression of the Conciliar teaching that Mary *is* the Mother of God. The original Greek text, upon which the Latin poetry is based, contains these two phrases: *kexāritōmena* ("one having been favored"), and *kurius meta su* ("the Lord is with you"). The technique was designed to allow the devotee to poetically experience the text by hearing the names of Mary and Jesus. The structure of this Latin form of *Hesychistic* prayer, recalling the presence of God to Mary, places oneself alongside Mary to experience the comfort of her name, but above all as a proclamation of the victory of Jesus.

The Rosary: A Prayer of Victory

IN the twentieth century, English Catholic writers have addressed this Marian topic in a very homey style. Among them are John Henry Cardinal Newman, Caryll Houselander, G.K. Chesterton, Gerald Vann, O.P., Hubert van Zeller, O.S.B., and most recently Basil

Cardinal Hume, O.S.B., the late Archbishop of Westminster. Notes from his spiritual diary were compiled into a series of pastoral essays, published under the title *To Be a Pilgrim*. Here are his words:

> Prayer to Our Lady is part of the Christian instinct. It must be part of ours. It would be folly to neglect that prayer which has been said down the ages, the Holy Rosary. That prayer has its own attraction and its own value. If we find, as we sometimes do, that we are neglecting the Rosary, then a feast of Our Blessed Lady is a strong reminder and a prompting of our determination to take it up again. *The faithful who pray the Rosary always remain close to the Virgin Mary, and those who are close to her can only draw closer to her Divine Son.*

Let it be recalled, from above, that the Crucifixion of Jesus, like all other Roman crucifixions, was intended to obliterate not only the life of the victim on the cross but also the *name* of the one condemned as a criminal to such a death. Shouts of *"momser"* were hurled at Jesus by the crowd at Calvary, in the presence of His Mother. His name, like His life, was intended to die. Yet the climax of this Marian *Hesychistic* prayer is evangelical, i.e., "good news." The center of the poem is the proclamation of the Resurrection of Jesus, Whose name, like His person, lives on after His death. The "Angelic Salutation" or "the Marian formula," especially because it was poetic, was easily memorized. The vocal recitation of it makes for true prayer, which is, after all, the lifting up of the mind and heart to God.

The Rosary: A Crown of Glory

THE poetry of this prayer enjoyed special popularity in the Celtic monasticism of the sixth century C.E. Archaeology and anthropology provide insight into the formulation of the Rosary as a tactile instrument of prayer. From the time of St. Patrick, Irish monks were dedicated to the worship of God through the daily recitation of the 150 Psalms of David. Not connected to the monasticism of the East or the Benedictine tradition of the continent of Europe, Consecrated Religious of Ireland possessed a unique style for prayer in the monastery. It is highly notable that physically each monastic complex consisted of a series of concentric circles or crowns. At the heart of the colony was the church, the scriptorium, the school and its library, the kitchens and refectory, and some facilities for bathing and laundry.

In the first circle lived celibate clergy or monks; the second circle contained quarters for men who did not profess vows but lived dedicated lives of supportive service to the mission of the monastery and its ministry. These individuals were freer to come and go from the compound in order to conduct the monastic business. In some monasteries, the third circle was occupied by consecrated virgins or widows, nuns. Although enclosed, these too participated in the total life of the monastery, maintaining themselves modestly.

A fourth circle might be made up of a family of maidens, non-vowed devotees of the nuns, mainly young girls not yet married who provided supportive service. Widows were found among their company also. Like their male counterparts, they too had greater freedom to come and go in the compound. A fifth circle was often occupied by married couples and families, who had, as a whole, pledged a covenant of identity with the monastery, to pray, to study, to support its mission, and to assist with material and agricultural needs.

Some monasteries were completely male. Some were female. Usually lay people were attached to all monasteries, and Celtic monastic life included them. Inevitably, there was an outer circle, occupied by mercenary soldiers to protect the inhabitants from Viking invaders or other mercenaries who were inspired by Druids, as well as thieves and rival clans. The Rosary's development is connected to the circular pattern of life, which the early Irish Christians devised for themselves. It comes as no surprise, then, that from the very earliest days the round chaplet, or *cabana*, became an instrument of popular piety.

Given this Irish monastic structure with its unique composition of personnel, while the Consecrated Religious chanted the 150 Psalms of David, others, not schooled in Latin, joined them, at first, by the pious recitation of the Lord's Prayer 150 times. It is only natural that the Our Father should be deemed the perfect counterpart to the Psalms, since both were recognized as the inspired text of Sacred

Scripture. Already, the Lord's Prayer was deemed to be the compendium of Jesus' teaching about the Kingdom of God; after all it was His personal prayer.

Archaeology shows that the first chaplets consisted of 150 pebbles or seashells. Some instruments consisted of 150 knots of rope. Others were composed of 150 blocks of wood. Eventually, the blocks of wood gave way to beaded chains of a type and style which we use today. The style and form of the Rosary evolved; the 150 Our Fathers became 150 repetitions of the Angelic Salutation, the *Ave Maria*. Legend places St. Dominic and his companions as the watershed in the evolution of this devotion, since it is said that they presented a stable formula by teaching the contemplation of the Joyful, Sorrowful, and Glorious Mysteries to the rhythm of the repetitive prayer, the *Ave Maria*.

The Our Father was now recited only five times. Eventually, the *Glory Be to the Father (Gloria Patri)*, also known as the Trinitarian Doxology, was added at the end of each Mystery. On occasions when devotion for the dead was celebrated, often the *Gloria* was replaced by the words *"May eternal rest shine on them, O Lord, and let a perpetual light shine upon them."* Certainly a recognized, universally received formula is identified with St. Dominic, circa 1208 C.E. This brought an end to the evolution of the Rosary in the Dark Ages. That formula was confirmed by another Dominican, Michael Ghislieri, O.P. Cardinal Ghislieri was elected Pope in 1566 and took the name Pius V. He was canonized a Saint in 1712.

In 1571, the Turkish fleet threatened Christianity and challenged a formation of the Holy League in the Gulf of Corinth. The Holy League consisted of troops from Venice, Spain, and the Papal States. Pope Pius V begged the prayerful assistance of all the Christian nations to halt the progress of the Turks who had almost defeated the Knights of Malta at Fort St. Elmo in 1565.

Then the Pope ordered the celebration of the Forty Hours Devotion at Rome and invited continuous universal recitation of the Rosary throughout Western Christendom. When Don Juan of Austria defeated the Turkish fleet under the Sign of the Cross and with the invocation of "Mary Help of Christians," Pope Pius V confirmed the Dominican mode of reciting the Rosary, and established October 7 as a day of commemoration of the event. He called it the Feast of Our Lady of Victory. It was his immediate successor, Pope Gregory XIII (1572-1610), who established the day as the Feast of Our Lady of the Rosary. Evidence indicates Pius V composed the prayer which would become the Collect of the Mass for the Feast of Our Lady of the Rosary. Today, this same prayer is recited at the end of every Rosary: *"Grant, we beseech You, that meditating upon these Mysteries we may imitate what they contain and obtain what they promise. . . ."*

The Popes and the Rosary

REFLECTING upon this formula, Pope John Paul II today confirms the expressions of intent contained therein, placing special emphasis on imitating the content of the Mystery and obtaining its promise.

The Pontiff also encourages modern and spontaneous expressions of local custom and personal need. The teaching of the Prayer of the Rosary is certainly meant to provide universally for the Pilgrim People of God:

Such a final prayer could take on a legitimate variety of forms, as indeed it already does. In this way, the Rosary can be better adapted to different spiritual traditions and different Christian communities. It is to be hoped, then, that appropriate formulas will be widely circulated, after due pastoral discernment and possibly after experimental use in centers and shrines, particularly devoted to the Rosary, so that the People of God may benefit from an abundance of authentic spiritual riches and find nourishment for their personal contemplation (*RVM*, no. 35).

In this Apostolic Letter, Pope John Paul II confirms the instructions of his predecessors regarding the Rosary. Already he has mentioned his proximate predecessors Pope John XXIII and Pope Paul VI. He also made a laudatory reference to Leo XIII, who promulgated his own encyclical *Supremi Apostolatus Officio* in 1883, in which he proposed the Rosary as "an effective spiritual weapon against the evils afflicting society." In other encyclicals, Pope Leo XIII wrote: "Among persons, families, and whole nations where the practice of the Rosary is honored, we will not fear that ignorance or pernicious evil will destroy the faith." By making continued similar statements, Pope Leo XIII reflected the widespread popularity of the Rosary in the nineteenth century, as evidenced by shrines such as Lourdes and La Salette. Likewise, in the widespread migrations of Catholics during his Pontificate, the Rosary was practically the only instrument of faith which could accompany them.

In 1912, as the Titanic was sinking, a group of Irish immigrants, all from the same village, prayed the Rosary until the moment when the ship was submerged. The only survivor from that group, who later became a Sister of Mercy of Worcester, Massachusetts, Sister Patricia Marie, told her story. The Rosary comforted these teenagers against a cruel and cold fate. The Rosary went with Italians to Argentina, with Polish and Slavic people to Wilkes-Barre, Pennsylvania, and Cleveland, Ohio, and with German refugees of the *Kulturkampf* to the plains of Kansas and Iowa. Meanwhile, among the laity in China, Rosary groups were the public identification of their Catholic faith.

By referring to his predecessors, John Paul II indicates his personal witness to the efficacy of this powerful prayer in Church tradition. He stands alongside Pius V, Gregory XIII, Leo XIII, John XXIII, and Paul VI. Unlike those others, who wrote in the Roman jargon of stylized sentences, Pope John Paul offers his personal witness: "How many graces have I received in these years from the Blessed Virgin through the Rosary: *Magnificat anima mea Dominum!* ['My soul magnifies the Lord!'] I wish to lift up my thanks to the Lord in the words of His Most Holy

Mother, under whose protection I have placed my Petrine ministry: *Totus Tuus"* (*RVM*, no. 2).

By reflecting upon the significance and early development of the Rosary, one learns that it is a repetitive prayer which has counterparts in other religious traditions. The repetition implies the hearing of the names of Jesus and Mary, and is an expression of Christian reverence for them. It is an expression of the Incarnation of Jesus as Son of God and Son of Mary. It is a recognition of the Resurrection and an acknowledgment of the continued presence of God. While it is a vocal prayer, it leads everyone to a mystical awareness to look beneath the surface of life, and to find out what is really there. To examine the contemplative side of the Rosary, it is now necessary to look at its structure and to turn once again to its evolution.

Structure of the Rosary

CURIOUSLY, in *Rosarium Virginis Mariae*, Pope John Paul II did not mention the Letter of Pope Pius XI, *Inclytam ac Perillustrem* ("Glorious and Illustrious"). In that papal document of the 1930s, Pope Pius had written: "Above all, the Rosary nourishes the Catholic faith, which grows stronger by meditation on the Sacred Mysteries and elevates the mind to truths revealed by God." That Pontiff went on to say: "The Rosary enlivens the hope for the things above which endure forever. As we meditate on *the glances of Jesus Christ and His Mother,* we see heaven opened, and are heartened, and are striving to gain the eternal home."

Finally he wrote: "How could we not be made more fervent by the Rosary? We meditate on the suffering and death of His afflicted Mother. Will we not make a return of love for the love received?"

These remarks of Achille Ratti, otherwise known as Pius XI, remain valuable. This particular Pope had to maintain his Pontificate at the precipice of "the Age of the Dictators." He saw around him the persecution of Catholics in Mexico, Portugal, Spain, Germany, Italy, and the Soviet Union. When Hitler came to visit Mussolini, Pius XI withdrew from Rome so as not even to be near them. He did not live to see the onset of the Second World War, but he knew it was coming. He offered the Rosary, especially to the laity, as a means of protection and a consolation when a Christian would be victimized, arrested, tortured, and imprisoned.

Even when the instrument of the Rosary would be stripped away, along with every other Sacramental channel of grace, heroes and heroines did continue to pray it, using their fingers and toes. This was certainly true in testimonies regarding the martyred Alfred Delp, S.J., the Blessed Sister Restituda of Vienna, and the heroic survivor Gereon Karl Goldman, O.F.M. In the Cold War years, those same words of encouragement became part of the Constitution of the lay-inspired movements such as Catholic Action, the Young Christian Workers, and the Legion of Mary. At that time the specter of Communism fell everywhere, achieving its greatest success in Asia. In 1949, when all resistance against Communism in China ceased, persecutions against Catholics commenced. The words of

Pius XI did not go unheeded: "Will we not make a return of love for the love received?"

As a Passionist, I was privileged to know many members of my community who endured solitary confinement coupled with torture for many years. For me, the most notable of them were Bishop Cuthbert O'Gara, C.P., and Fathers Paul Joseph Ubinger, C.P., Justin Garvey, C.P., and Marcellus White, C.P. All of them survived on the continual recitation of the Rosary. I remember well the late Bishop O'Gara spending long hours in the Passionist Monastery Choir, reciting his Rosary over and over again. In his later years, the late Ignatius Cardinal Kung came to the Passionist Monastery in West Hartford, Connecticut, for some days of retreat. At night, he could be heard calling out as he relived, in his sleep, the dreams of his thirty-three years of solitary confinement. Until the day of his death, he took the Rosary to bed with him as his only source of consolation.

The same could be said of Sister Theresa Joseph Lung, C.S.J., of Hunan Province, who was separated from all clergy and religious for more than thirty years This heroic woman of the Baden Sisters of St. Joseph used her Rosary to form Christian communities, to catechize, and to baptize. When she was reunited with her community in 1983, it was discovered that she used the lessons and the method of the Rosary to establish a new Religious Community of women in Nanjing. When she died some years later, there were nineteen young women who followed a Rule of Life based upon the significance of the Rosary.

Today, in North Korea, where there are no Catholic clergy or religious at all, Catholics assemble on Sunday, as they have done for fifty years, read the Scriptures, make a Spiritual Communion with the Masses being celebrated around the world that day, and recite all fifteen decades of the Rosary together. These are the lessons of Pius XI, who claimed that the Rosary recaptured the look of Mary and Jesus at each other, "a return of love for the love received."

The encyclical of Pope Pius XI also makes a fitting prologue to *Rosarium Virginis Mariae* because it confirms the development of the Rosary along the parallel history of the Dominican Order. Reference to *Inclytam ac Perillustrem* enables the scholar to sort out the evidence of the foregoing, cited above, to develop an idea of the significance of how the Rosary evolved. Pius XI wrote:

> Among the weapons St. Dominic used to convert the heretics, the most efficacious, as the faithful well know, was the Marian Rosary, the practice of which, taught by the Blessed Virgin herself, has so widely spread throughout the Catholic world. Now where does the efficacy and power of this manner of praying come from? Certainly from the very Mysteries of the Divine Redeemer which we contemplate and piously meditate so that we may rightly say that the Marian Rosary contains the root and foundation on which the Order of St. Dominic depends in order to procure perfection of life of its own members and the salvation of other men.

This statement from a Pope, a famous and expertly trained historian and antiquarian, affirms the figure of St. Dominic Guzman as the watershed in the development of the Rosary. The significance of the Rosary for popular piety and personal sanctification is underscored in 215 Papal Bulls, Decrees, Encyclicals, and Apostolic Letters. Since 1261, when Pope Alexander IV confirmed the Rosary as a valid devotion, thirty-nine other Popes have written to continue the tradition.

The Evolution of the Rosary

A S has been cited above, the Angelic Salutation, then the *Ave Maria,* emerged as a Christian prayer at the time of the Council of Ephesus in 431. By the end of the first Christian millennium, the use of the Hail Mary was an accepted Latin form of *Hesychistic* prayer. At the same time, the chaplet of Our Fathers as an instrument of accompaniment to the Monastic Office of the Irish Religious Communities had been replaced by Hail Marys.

In the eleventh century, devotion to Mary spread in Western Europe. Statues of the Madonna were erected at various medieval shrines. There the Marian Salutation was recited aloud repetitiously before statues, icons, and pictures of the Blessed Mother. St. Peter Damian, a cardinal, bishop, and papal legate, who preceded St. Dominic by more than a century, is identified as the principal promoter of public devotion at Marian shrines. In particular, his position as a diplomat led him across Europe where he promoted the devotion of the Angelic Salutation at Marian shrines everywhere he went.

The shift to the new millennium of course saw new expressions of style, and therefore mutations. Coming now was the age of chivalry, an age of hunger for popular expressions of piety among the laity, the age of the friars (Franciscan, Dominican, Augustinian, and Carmelite), the age of the university (Padua, Paris, and Oxford) and the great cathedrals (Cologne, Utrecht, Toledo, and Lisbon). As all of these emerged, the Marian focus grew and deepened; Mary's patronage was sought because, as is written by Sister Benedicta Ward: "[It was the universal belief] that the Virgin Mary had been assumed into heaven. . . . There was no body to be venerated and no central shrine to house it." Previously, popular devotion focused on relics and pilgrimages to sacred sites.

In conjunction with the age of chivalry, devotion to the Assumption of Mary gave her the title "Lady." Mary's Ladyship was affiliated with and depended upon Christ's Lordship. Images of her had always depicted her in the royal blue or purple of a Byzantine empress, but now those images were adorned with crowns of gold. Jewels decorated her clothing. For she was deemed to be royal, and, as monarchs declared their sovereignty, Lady Mary was seen as a counterpart to the Lord Jesus, and above time and place, although she was *from* time and space. She was, therefore, honored in various medieval centers of piety under the title "Our Lady" or "Notre Dame." Thus, we find such Marian centers as Notre

Dame de Paris, Notre Dame de Chartres, and Our Lady of Eversham.

The Cistercian Order, a newer, simpler, but more strict expression of Benedictine Monasticism, emerged directly at the juncture between the eleventh and the twelfth century. Its three founders, Robert, Alberic, and Stephen, dedicated this new endeavor to the protection of "Our Lady." To this day, most abbeys of the Cistercian and Trappist Order bear that title, e.g., Our Lady of the Redwood, Our Lady of the Lake, Our Lady of Gethsemane, etc. The foremost promoter of the Marian Cistercian spirit was St. Bernard of Clairvaux (1090-1153). Known as "The Last of the Fathers," he was also known as "Mary's Faithful Bernard." Bernard specifically preached the Assumption of Mary and the corollary title of "Her Ladyship." It is he who called her "Mediatrix of Graces" and "Star of the Sea."

Bernard's many discourses on Mary comprise the first complete treatise of Mariology. The best historical appreciation of Bernard's influence upon the development of Marian devotion was recalled by Pope Pius XII, who wrote an encyclical about Bernard in the 1950s. Bernard's clever use of language played upon the Latin name of Mary and the Latin word for ocean or sea, *"mare."* Through cleverly devised rhetoric, Bernard has left posterity with this gem of his mysticism. He wrote that *"mare"* could be interpreted to mean "Star of the Sea" and admirably suits her as the Virgin Mother. "When all was still, and the world was in quiet at night, Your Almighty Word leapt down" (Introit of the Midnight Mass).

Bernard's sense of appropriateness in this comparison of Mary as a star becomes clear when he indicates that a star sends out rays without detriment to itself. Therefore, he wrote: "So did the Virgin bring forth her Child without injury to her integrity, and as the rays emitted do not diminish the brightness, so neither did the Child born of her tarnish the beauty of Mary's virginity" (Writings of St. Bernard, Homily II, *Missus est*). Bernard's personal transparency and his skilled oratory moved the crowds at shrines and cathedrals to new Marian fervor.

Reference has already been made to the formalization and the promotion of the Rosary by St. Dominic in the thirteenth century. By this time, the faithful carried flowers to the statues of Mary and oftentimes, especially during processions, the statue was crowned with a flower coronet. Then as now, the most favored flower and the most admired was the rose. It takes little imagination then to take the name of the Rosary. Circles had been symbols since the fifth century. It is important to recall here the original structure of the *Ave Maria*, for during the repetitiveness of the Angelic Salutation, only the Joyful Mysteries of the Rosary, i.e., events associated with the Annunciation and the Nativity of Jesus, were points of meditation.

In the fourteenth century, a more formal and even more normative structure for saying the Rosary came into place. The second part of the *Ave Maria*, as we now know it ("Holy Mary, Mother of God . . .") was added. The decision to begin each Mystery with the recitation of an "Our Father" was taken; likewise the Trinitarian Doxology "Glory Be to the Father . . ." was added at the end of the Mystery. Finally, the Sorrowful and Glorious Mysteries were added to the Rosary. This definitive structure was promoted across Europe through the zealous efforts of the Venerable Alain of Roche, O.P., who preached the efficacy of the Rosary. The medieval evolution of the Rosary ceased in 1572, when Pope Pius V declared it an efficacious devotion of the Church in its contemporary form.

The Teaching of Pope John Paul II

THE publication of the Apostolic Letter *Rosarium Virginis Mariae* displays the innovation of Pope John Paul II. Like St. Bernard, he speaks of this devotion as "the blessed Rosary of Mary, sweet chain linking us to God" (*RVM*, no. 39). Like St. Pius V and Pope Pius XI, he has written: "At times when Christianity itself seemed under threat, its deliverance was attributed to the power of this prayer, and Our Lady of the Rosary was acclaimed as the one whose intercession brought salvation" (*RVM*, no. 39).

Further, Pope John Paul II affirmed the fourteenth-century addition for the recitation of the Our Father and the Trinitarian Doxology as part of each Mystery. Of the Lord's Prayer, he has written: "It is natural for *the mind to be lifted up toward the Father*. In each of His Mysteries, Jesus always leads us to the Father, for as He rests in the Father's bosom (cf. Jn 1:18), He is continually turned toward Him (*RVM*, no. 32). This relationship to the Father naturally invites the concept of communion or *"koinonia."* It recalls the nature and mission of the Church and the fruit of Baptism.

One is enabled to call God "Father" with all the implications that *Abba* (the Aramaic term for it used by Jesus) implies (Rom 8:15; Gal 4:6). Further, every Christian receives brotherhood from Christ, assuring His protection in our life's work and participation in His Mysteries. A bond between brothers and sisters in the faith is assured. One's neighbor ought not to be one's enemy. One's enemy is also one's neighbor. The gaze at the Father contained in the Lord's Prayer ensures the cardinal Virtues of faith, hope, and love as components of the grace of personal friendship and friendships.

By the attention that he gives to the Trinitarian Doxology, the "Glory Be to the Father," Pope John Paul II affirms also the poetic mysticism of the fourteenth century, not to speak of the prayer *formulae* of the catacombs. He calls this the high point of contemplation. Since the time of St. Augustine of Hippo, the definition of "glory" has been *clara notitia cum laude* ("clear knowledge with praise"). The Pontiff therefore expresses: "Trinitarian Doxology is the goal of *all* Christian contemplation" (*RVM*, no. 34; *emphasis, mine*). Each Christian life is a pilgrimage, and if taken to the end through reflection and the imagination, one comes to realize himself/herself before the Mysteries of the Trinity.

Finally, the Pontiff acknowledges the importance of the ten Hail Marys for each Mystery. He states: "This is the most substantial element in the Rosary and also the one that makes it a Marian prayer *par excellence"* (*RVM*, no. 33). In light of the evidence above, when the "Hail Mary" is properly understood, it becomes clear that its Marian context is not opposed to its Christological content. The juxtaposition of the names of Jesus and Mary "actually emphasizes and increases [the Christological character]" (*RVM*, no. 33).

Silence: The Method of the Rosary

THE content of previous sections has afforded the opportunity of reviewing the insights of the Second Vatican Council regarding the Christian faith. Many of those insights, in fact, flow from theological developments in the nineteenth century. In general, contemporary scholars have pretty much agreed that John Henry Newman (1800-1890) was the most formidable voice regarding theological insight, combining the evidence of antiquities, the authenticity of the devotional life, pastoral application, theological methodology, and the mission of the Church. His publications and his letters are all veritable treasures. His language combines personal innovation with the content of Christian Tradition. Therefore, it is appropriate to turn to Newman to understand the uniqueness of the Rosary and its composition.

Shortly before his death, someone approached Cardinal Newman in his Birmingham Oratory to express a doubt about the usefulness of the recitation of the Creed at Mass. Newman was always a simple priest and eminently approachable. His incisive mind and his ecclesiastical dignity as Cardinal did not impede personal contact with the faithful. In fact, he lived and wrote within the Birmingham Oratory, as well as celebrated Mass, preached, and heard Confessions in the Oratory Church. He also taught the students who attended the Oratory Grammar School. He never lost the common touch.

Newman listened patiently to his inquirer's complaint: "Is it not useless and boring to recite or sing the words of the *Credo* at Mass? [I believe in God the Father Almighty. . . .] After all," the man continued, "this is not a prayer, but a formula of expressions of the Council of Nicea (325 C.E.). It really is not addressed to God; for that matter, it is not really addressed to anyone in particular; it is unparalleled to any Christian prayer. It does not even end with the usual words *'through Christ our Lord. Amen.'* "

Newman replied with the wisdom which he derived from the expertise of his native field of Patristic Studies. The Creed is a litany of adoration of the Trinity and lists, before the Face of God, praise for all the elements of the Christ-event, which is known as the Redemption. Such a formula is in conformity with St. Augustine's definition of glory, already cited, *clara notitia cum laude* ("clear knowledge with praise") and St. Basil's representation of *Martyrion* ("witness"). Thus did Newman represent the spirituality of both West and East from the consensus of the Patristic Age. The *Ave Maria* is likewise a prayer form similar to the structure of the Creed. It replays before the Face of God those blessed words which inaugurated the Christ-event. The mere memory and recitation of them is an act of gratitude for the gift of the Incarnation.

In *Rosarium Virginis Mariae,* Pope John Paul II recognizes the uniqueness of the *Ave Maria* formula. Like the Creed, it too is a product of the Patristic Age. He identifies its two panels: "The first part of the *Hail Mary,* drawn from the words spoken to Mary by the Angel Gabriel and by St. Elizabeth, is *a contemplation in adoration* of the Mystery accomplished in the Virgin of Nazareth. These words express the *wonder* of heaven and earth; they could be said [also] to give a glimpse of *God's* own wonderment as He contemplates His 'masterpiece'—the Incarnation of the Son in the womb of the Virgin Mary" (*RVM,* no. 33; *emphasis, mine*). The Pontiff, following his 1999 *Letter to the Artists*, juxtaposes the Annunciation, as recorded in Luke, with the Creation account from the Book of Genesis. On the seventh day of Creation, God expressed jubilant amazement, wonder, and pleasure at all that He had made, and the Old Testament scribe reports: "God saw all that He had made, and it was very good" (Gn 1:31).

St. Luke reports in his account of the Visitation that Elizabeth assumes the role of a prophetess, and therefore she is seen to be "of God." Elizabeth says: "Blessed are you among women . . ." (Lk 1:42). Her words are accompanied by a spontaneous gesture, the leap of the unborn child in her womb. Such an event is consistent with other prophetic acts, wrought by God in the accounts of the Old Testament prophets. Such acts affect or demonstrate what the words predict. In this case, Elizabeth's womb, according to Jewish cosmology, represents the whole event of the Creation. Mary too is a prophet. Says Pope John Paul II: "Mary's prophecy here finds its fulfillment: 'Henceforth, all generations *will* call *me* blessed' (Lk 1:48)" (*RVM*, no. 33; *emphasis, mine*).

The first panel of the Marian prayer is very much akin to Newman's explanation of the Creed. It too is a litany of the extraordinary deeds of God before the face of God in order to render Him praise. The words "Hail Mary, full of grace" are an angelic proclamation. Again, according to Jewish cosmology, they too represent the presence of God. Newman reflects this in his own Marian meditations, not only citing Gabriel but invoking Michael and including the Angelic apparition to the shepherds of the fields on the night of Jesus' birth:

> The two archangels who have a special office in the Gospel are St. Michael and St. Gabriel—and both of them are associated in the history of the Incarnation with Mary: St. Gabriel, when the Holy Ghost [sic] came down upon her; and St. Michael, when the Divine Child was born. . . .
>
> St. Gabriel hailed her as full of grace, and as "blessed among women," and announced to her that the Holy Ghost would come down upon her, and that she would bear a son, who would be the Son of the Highest. . . .

Of St. Michael's ministry to her, on the birth of that Divine Son, we learn in the Apocalypse, written by the Apostle St. John. . . .

Newman's point is that the presence of the angels throughout the Infancy Narrative presents us with the appropriate expression of *their* perennial prayer: *"Sanctus, Sanctus, Sanctus"* ("Holy, Holy, Holy").

The angels observed the Christ-event as the work of the Sovereign Creator God. Their words of praise are intended to inspire awe, from generation to generation, from deep within the Church, from deep within the heart of each believer. Pope John Paul II has therefore composed what I believe to be the most meaningful sentences in this entire Apostolic Letter:

The center of gravity in the *Hail Mary*, the hinge as it were which joins its two parts, is *the name of Jesus.* Sometimes, in hurried recitation, this center of gravity can be overlooked, and with it the connection to the Mystery of Christ being contemplated. Yet it is precisely the emphasis given *to the name of* Jesus and *to His Mystery that is the sign of a meaningful and fruitful recitation of the Rosary (RVM, no. 33; emphasis, mine).*

The repetition of the Angelic Salutation, the Elizabethan greeting, and the name of Jesus itself are the best expressions of praise because the words come from the heart of the Mystery.

Pope John Paul II explains: "Highlighting the name of Christ by the addition of a clause referring to the Mystery being celebrated . . . is at once *a profession of faith* and an aid in concentrating our meditation, since it facilitates the process of assimilation to the Mystery of Christ inherent in the repetition of the *Hail Mary*" (*RVM*, no. 33). The Pontiff reiterates the importance of repeating the name of Jesus, "the *only name* given to us by which we may hope for salvation" (*RVM*, no. 33). Again, he speaks of the juxtaposition of the names of Jesus and Mary so that "we set out on a path of assimilation meant to help us enter more deeply into the life of Christ" (*RVM*, no. 33).

All of this we have already observed as we have come to recognize the evidence of history: The *Ave Maria* evolved in order that through its repetition one may be *comforted* by the Holy Names and taken into the unique relationship between the two persons, Jesus and Mary, whom those names identify.

The Method of Pope John Paul II

IN order to make the joy of this contemplation accessible to everyone, the Pontiff has two remedies. The headlines have already announced the new set of Mysteries known as the *Luminous Mysteries of the Rosary*, an innovation which draws closer attention to Jesus in His person and in His message. Yet the commentators have paid scarce attention to Pope John Paul II's *own* method for reciting the Rosary. Just as the Eastern *Hesychistic* prayer is founded upon the slow repetition of words accompanied by a physical technique of the body, so too does the Pope invite the Rosary not to be a hurried, vocal activity. It too has a sense of rhythm that is fed by recollection. It too is a prayer of the heart, and calls for the use of the imagination and for self-composure during the exercise.

Pope John Paul II proposes a three-step technique for reciting the Rosary. The first of these is announcing each Mystery out loud, even if just to oneself, if convenient. The words themselves provide the focus. Like the visual images found in Catholic culture, such as the crucifix, icons, and statues, the words of the Mystery are intended to sharpen the attention and to recall the "composition of place," as already referred to above by citing the teaching of St. Ignatius Loyola. The Rosary definitely is about the appeal to the senses. The entire prayer of the Rosary invites a certain passivity so that one may *experience* the grace interiorly.

For pragmatic Americans, this concept appears foreign. The English-speaking world is oriented toward accomplishment and therefore is utilitarian. However, Christianity is about the effectiveness of God's grace, and therefore we pray: "May God Who has begun this good work in us bring it to fulfillment."

The history of Christian spirituality is telling. Passivity is effective *only if one allows God to speak.* The Pope advises that without keeping this principle in mind the Rosary's continued repetition will only give rise to *ennui,* i.e., boredom, detachment, an "I don't care" attitude. In order to prevent this, Pope John Paul II recommends reading passages of

Scripture in accompaniment with the presentation of each Mystery. This method, too, feeds the imagination and the intellect. It inspires insight. Insight comforts. The image of the whole Jesus-Mystery, God's intervention in human history and His action in Christ, is really at the heart of the prayer of the Rosary. The Rosary is an appreciation of God.

Finally, the Pope's method calls for silence. Here he is specific. Here he invites a pause after the Mystery has been announced and the biblical passage has been reviewed. This is a moment of focus, important in every human activity. The fruit of focus is effectiveness. For this cause, the Pope has specifically written: "A discovery of the importance of silence is one of the secrets of practicing contemplation and meditation. One drawback of a society dominated by technology and the mass media is the fact that silence becomes increasingly difficult to achieve. Just as moments of silence are recommended in the Liturgy, so too in the recitation of the Rosary it is fitting to pause briefly after listening to the Word of God, while the mind focuses on the content of a particular Mystery" (*RVM*, no. 31).

Because it relies on images, meditation points to poetry. At first the realization of this fact may prove daunting, but eventually it is a comfort. It is certainly the fulfillment of a biblical mandate: "Be filled with the Spirit, speaking to yourselves in songs, hymns, and spiritual psalms, singing and making melody in your heart" (Eph 5:19). Silence stirs up personal images. It can recall distractions, consolations, and desolations from one's past experience. It places everything before God: memorable moments of self-knowledge, affections of sorrow and love, conversations with the Divine Presence, and sometimes just simply no thoughts or feelings at all, a kind of emptiness which is an invitation to God to come and fill the void. An individual who is serious about his or her life, in perpetual quest to draw analogies from the everyday world, is no stranger to the recollection and silence which the Pope calls for.

Of course, all of this is expressed in the second panel of the *Ave Maria:* "Holy Mary, Mother of God, pray for us sinners now and at the hour of our death. Amen." One's actions, memories, and aspirations perpetually seek the mercy of God, which is always available from the intercession of Jesus, accompanied by the prayers of Mary.

Personally, I have many images of this type of silence. In the past, on two occasions I was secretary to two different Cardinals. Both of them had very busy schedules. As I drove one or the other of them from place to place, they inevitably pulled out their Rosary for a few moments of prayer. In both high school and college, I had friends who, on the surface of life, did not appear to be particularly pious. Yet, I found them, boys and girls alike, pausing to recite their Rosary. I see it today. Businessmen on the subway, patients in the waiting room of a doctor's office, actors, physicians, journalists, lawyers going about their day with a Rosary or a Rosary ring discreetly hidden in their hand.

My most poignant memory is of a man who was my father's best friend. His name was Thomas Donahoe. I chose him to be my sponsor for Confirmation, and I always called him "Uncle Tom." He was a genius of an upholsterer. Among his many fine works was the fabric for "Falling Water," Frank Lloyd Wright's masterpiece. Uncle Tom taught handicapped people the technique of his unique craft. He found the time to serve as consultant to all three major department stores of Pittsburgh. He was granted a Master of Fine Arts degree, but he never actually moved beyond the eighth grade. He gave shrewdly and untiringly to the poor of Pittsburgh. Never was the Rosary out of his hand, even when it also contained hammer and nails. He was much admired and he had untiring energy, and he was not ashamed to say he found his strength in his own discreet way of reciting the Rosary.

The Rosary and the Call to Holiness

AT the conclusion of the Apostolic Letter *Rosarium Virginis Mariae,* Pope John Paul II referred to the Rosary as a prayer "so easy and so rich" which truly deserves to be rediscovered by the Christian Community. In exhorting the Church to appreciate anew the time-honored tradition of the Rosary, the Pontiff calls upon the witness of many. Most specifically, the Pontiff invited trained theologians to help him explain the depth of the Rosary and its potential as a rich source of comfort and grace. He said:

> I also place my trust in you, theologians:
> by your sage and rigorous reflection, rooted in

the Word of God [Holy Scripture], and sensitive to the lived experience of the Christian people, may you help them to discover the biblical foundations, the spiritual riches, and the pastoral value of this traditional prayer (*RVM,* no. 43).

Such a direct charge to theologians regarding an act of piety is an innovation. Theologians are often seen as personally remote, professionally preoccupied, and devoid of the pastoral touch. Theirs can be a world of books, research, lectures, and academic politics. However, that image has been set aside by the Second Vatican Council. The Council has left a legacy that is valid on many levels. Its clearest mandate is the reiteration of "the Universal call to holiness." This is the heart of the Mystery of the Church:

It is therefore quite clear that *all Christians in any state or walk of life are called to the fullness of Christian life* and to the perfection of love, and *by this holiness a more human manner of life is fostered* also in earthly society. In order to reach this perfection, the faithful should use the strength dealt out to them by Christ's gift, so that, *following in His footsteps and conformed to His image,* doing the Will of God in everything, they may wholeheartedly devote themselves to the glory of God and to the service of their neighbor. Thus, the holiness of the People of God will grow in fruitful abundance, as is *clearly shown in the history of the*

Church through the life of so many Saints
(*Lumen Gentium*, no. 40; *emphasis, mine*).

This passage, taken from the *Dogmatic Constitution on the Church*, focuses the Pope's appeal for the input of theologians regarding the Rosary. His invitation pertains to the development of the concept of "the Universal call to holiness." Such phrases, including Royal Priesthood of the Faithful, Principle of Collegiality, and Evangelization as the Church's Mission, climax the content of many movements within the life of the Roman Catholic Church, which began either in the waning days of the nineteenth century or the early years of the twentieth century.

Such movements are remembered by their endeavor, i.e., the missionary movement, the ecumenical movement, the liturgical movement, the catechetical movement, and, perhaps most significantly, the movement toward a lay spirituality and apostolate. This last category contributed most regarding the universal call to holiness, as presented by the Council Fathers in the setting of the Mystery of the Church. "In the Church, not everyone marches along the same path, *yet all are called to sanctity* and have obtained an equal privilege of faith through the justice of God" (cf. 2 Pet 1:1; *Lumen Gentium*, no. 32; *emphasis, mine*).

It is perhaps worthwhile to map out this development through some references to the early twentieth century. The theology of the Mystery of the Rosary is very closely associated with the spirituality of the laity, precisely because the laity are the vessels of the devotional life of the Church. This is what Newman meant by the *Sensus Fidelium* and what Pope John XXIII and Pope Paul VI meant by the phrase "signs of the times" in their encyclicals. It is about the richness the Church derives as it observes the prayers and devotional style of the faithful.

The Emergence of the Spirituality of the Laity in the Twentieth Century

IT is well known today that Edith Stein, a renowned philosopher of Jewish origin and also a Carmelite nun, perished in Auschwitz on August 9, 1942. After her conversion to the Catholic Church in the 1920s, Edith Stein worked as a teacher and lectured publicly as a representative of a kind of Christian feminism. She went all over Germany stressing the necessity of developing a vital spirituality for lay women. Her lectures in general addressed the importance of prayer and contemplation as a source of identity and strength for every woman, whether wife, mother, professional, or seamstress. She wrote about herself: "I do not take myself too seriously as a teacher, and I still have to smile when I have to put it down anywhere as my profession. But that does not hinder me from taking my responsibilities seriously, and so, in spirit and soul, I am deeply absorbed by them."

Edith Stein believed that all male professions were also a possibility for women; women, by reason of their gender, fulfill a task not only quantitatively but also qualitatively. In a series of discourses and articles collected under the title, *Essays on Woman,* she stated that the Christian commitment is personal union with the Redeemer and eternal contemplation of God. Christian commitment is a destiny that is both natural and supernatural. Although the experiences may differ, it is at the same time identical for men and women alike.

Western Civilization has always targeted human existence as some kind of family or community life. Community calls for the virtue of self-sacrifice, and *interior* growth as each person matures physically and experientially. Edith Stein, therefore, encouraged prayer because, like Albert Schweitzer, she believed that without concomitant human growth alongside the observable technical developments and social evolution of the twentieth century, Western civilization would be doomed unless the momentum of spirituality kept pace. Edith Stein wrote:

It depends on knowing one's way, and going to the source again and again. There is always a way open to each of the faithful: the way of prayer. Whoever sincerely believes in the words "Ask and you shall receive" is given consolation and courage to persevere in every need.

Clearly, Edith Stein proclaimed an active role for the Catholic lay woman and invited one and all to a life of active contemplation, reminding them that the Catholic Church belonged to everybody. In this cause for a lay spirituality in Germany, she was joined by two other famous authors, Gertrude von Le Fort and Ida Friederike Görres.

While Edith Stein and her companions campaigned for expressions of lay spirituality in Germany, other initiatives emerged across Europe. In Holland came the Society of the Grail. In Austria, a Society of Our Lady of the Way emerged. In Belgium, Joseph (later Cardinal) Cardijn organized the Young Christian Workers Movement. University students were invited to experience a deeper Christian spirituality through the Newman Movement. In Italy, Pope Pius XI encouraged young adults and graduate students to form "Catholic Action" to challenge the multiple pagan philosophies of Fascism.

In North America, Dorothy Day and Peter Maurin established the Catholic Worker Movement against Communism. The United States and Canada likewise experienced the influence of Baroness Katherine de Hueck. Probably the most influential of all, because it was so facile and so universal, was the Legion of Mary, founded in Ireland in 1921, and associated with the names of Frank Duff and Edele Quinn. The idea of kitchen spirituality, which was oriented toward the vocation of the homemaker, was addressed by Mary Perkins Ryan, Mary Reed Newland, and Katherine Burton.

Other outstanding intellectuals also contributed in their own way to the origins of a dialogue about the laity and Christianity. Their names and their ideas were very much present at the Second Vatican Council. They are Jacques Maritain, Étienne Gilson, and Christopher Dawson.

The name Vittorino Veronese is scarcely known today. Veronese, a doctor of law from the University of Padua, and the father of seven children, brought representatives of these movements as well as representatives of other initiatives together in 1951 with the First World Congress of the Lay Apostolate. This assembly convened in Rome. It reiterated three basic principles which had motivated a lay spirituality for more than a century: "The *primacy* of the spiritual; an *open and positive concept* of Catholicism (not a besieged fortress); and a *readiness to serve,* not to be served by the Church."

From there on, until the opening days of the Council, the Lay Apostolate Congresses sought the convergence of the many concepts of lay spirituality and addressed a wide variety of issues, some of them political, some practical, some educational. Essentially, however, it returned to *the vital place of personal prayer* in the formation of each lay vocation. An active participant in the Lay Apostolate Congresses was a zealous woman from Australia, Rosemary Goldie. It was she who would represent all these points as a lay auditor in the Second Vatican Council. Now presently retired in her native Australia, Miss Goldie remains a paragon of prayer, contemplation, and fervent engagement in the formation of lay leadership.

During the Second Vatican Council, Miss Goldie served directly with the young Bishop Karol Wojtyla in the draft of the *schema* regarding the laity, *Apostolicam Actuositatem.* Wojtyla was to serve as the only consistent Cardinal member of the Pontifical

Commission for the Laity, from the end of the Second Vatican Council until his election as Pope in 1978. It is no secret that Pope John Paul II and Miss Goldie have continued their many dialogues about spirituality as an expression of Baptismal Sonship and Royal Priesthood of the laity.

Holiness and the Council

A review of the speeches of the Council uncovers the penetrating insights in regard to this matter which came from Emile Joseph De Smedt, Bishop of Bruges, Belgium. Bishop De Smedt's intervention identified the vocation of the lay person directly with the Royal Priesthood of All Believers:

> With the help of Christ, mankind was given the power through human realities and labor to reach a supernatural goal and a share in that glory which He, as the first-born, began through His Resurrection and Ascension. In our day, by the layman's help, Christ plans, step-by-step, to complete this consecration of the world.

By Baptism, according to Bishop De Smedt, all are seconded to the universal priesthood of Christ, and no detail escapes the action of that grace, which flows from direct identity with Christ in his *priestly ministry, prophetic ministry, and kingly ministry.* A fellow countryman of De Smedt, Edward Schillebeeckx, put it this way: "On this account, through his Baptism, the faithful layman receives at the same time the charge to integrate the earthly purpose of his life into his *Com-*

munion embrace with God in Christ. Thus, the layman's earthly charge becomes part of his entirely God-centered attitude to life." The mandate perforce includes prayer in order to achieve that "God-centeredness" as seen by the Council Fathers.

This was also anticipated by one of the German women cited above. In a book of poetry, Gertrude von Le Fort wrote: *"The voice of the Church speaks: 'Come, my Children in the World, and be my witnesses; I have blessed you, and you must be a blessing.'"* The question remaining for each Christian is: "How do I wear the Blessing?"

Holiness: The Universal Call

THE answer comes from prayer and personal reflection as to the task of accepting the call to holiness as one's true, authentic, and only vocation. Most would be at odds to offer a definition of holiness. In the Christian dispensation, it *has* to be acknowledged that holiness is oriented toward the mature man or woman. The impetus to grow into maturity is in the heart of every human being. Parents teach their children to be responsible to fulfill their obligations, to contribute to the common good, to do and to be the worthiest that one can.

Maturity is definitely that goal. Being "grown up" is to have arrived at some sense of fulfillment. Holiness, first and foremost, is the exercise of justice, giving each, including oneself, what is due. Because the Christian is not ignorant of the Gospel and is redeemed by the blood of Christ, he or she accomplishes this justice out of a sense of the presence of God and from motives of love. There are three "debts" which are expressions of holiness.

The first of these is the acknowledgment of a partnership with God. God is Father, not only because He is Creator. God is Father also because He has taken each of the baptized to Himself, intimately, through the saving waters of Baptism. We are therefore invited to be like God, to be perfect as the Father in heaven is perfect. We know that the perfection of God lies in His love, "for God is love" (1 Jn 4:16). The accomplishment of every ideal is impossible for every individual, since everyone is fallible. God invites imitation of Him as we come to know Him, and to grow upward toward Him. This is the process of maturity.

It is an error to grow downward or away. God is incessantly at work. It is obvious that He did not construct the Creation and withdraw into its leisure. He is neither distant, nor detached, nor disinterested. Holiness consists in discerning the power and wonder of God's ways. God is the focus of the quest for holiness.

The second "debt" of holiness is oriented toward the Gospel value of community. Holiness is always oriented toward fellow men and women. It is a fact of life. This becomes more apparent all the time, first through ordinary contact. Through developing technologies and rapid social change, now at this point in history, it is apparent that our human existence is an interdependent entity. Gospel values call for ever more respect, even reverence, for those

whom we meet daily. A human life is, from concep-
tion until death, transformed by those we love and
those who love us, especially by God.

Tolerance, perforce, gives way to the recognition
and respect of pluriformity and individuality within the
human community. But something else is required—
notably, love. Love is from God. In fact, it is of God, for
God is love. Anyone who does not keep this concept in
mind is purely selfish. The ideal of personal fulfillment
through some kind of service which has never pene-
trated the process of his formation renders him narcis-
sistic. For such a person, charity is an alien term and
concept. But by His words (the parables) and by His
example (the miracles), Jesus *has* instructed His disciples and imitators of this basic truth of the Gospel: *the
individual standing next to me is my neighbor.* This is
the message of the Parable of the Good Samaritan (Lk
10:30-37).

Holiness recalls a passage from St. John: "Whoever
loves a brother or a sister *lives in the light,* and in such
a person there is no cause for stumbling" (1 Jn 2:10).
Holiness is associated with glory, which above we have
defined as "clear knowledge *with light."* The glory *of
the light* of Christ is never more magnified than
through an act of generosity, simple kindness, or silent
compassion. This constitutes the message of the Public
Life of Jesus. Hence, light, love, and revelation are united by the New Testament under the word "luminous."

Finally, holiness challenges the "debt" to oneself.
As Jesus instructed the crowds in Galilee and Judea,
one of His principal lessons was the value of *every*

human personality, including our own. Holiness of this kind is the most difficult because it is the rare person who wishes to spend time alone facing oneself. Holiness, however, is about the necessary maturity which accompanies that act of courage.

Each of us gets only a single life. Whatever one has done, or what has been done to a person, must be faced and accepted. It must be then turned over to God to be placed into His sacred plan. Surrendering to God in such a fashion may come to expression through self-forgiveness or self-affirmation. To do elsewise only adopts a pagan view of personal gratification, "Eat, drink, and be merry . . . etc." One could choose to wallow in grief, sin, or weakness. Holiness allows for none of this.

Holiness is light. It is the teaching of the Beloved Disciple that Christ Jesus is the light of life that penetrates the darkness. The Christian ideal pivots upon personal creativeness that is associated with moments of light, of insight, and of vision. Holiness invites every disciple of Christ to be ambitious, to leave a legacy, to attempt to do something everyday, to earn a good night's sleep. The deepest lesson of holiness is to accept this truth that through Baptism Christ is "in my heart by grace." I am not alone. He is with me. He is in me. Such an act requires courage, attentiveness, and recollection.

There is a direct affiliation between the Rosary and this understanding of a responsible God-centered life, which in the Christian dispensation is called holiness. Holiness is another word for that maturity in God and God's plan toward which every heart longs.

The Idea of the Luminous

THE phenomenon of light is a major component in the celebration of Christian liturgies. This has been so since the inception of Christianity itself in Jerusalem. The first Christians were also pious Jews. Lights, lamps, candelabrae, and candles were part of their heritage and were important aspects of Hebrew cultic practice since the time of Moses. During the period of the Exodus, the Ark of the Covenant was carried with reverence by day; a flame lighted by virgin oil rested before the Ark in the tent by night.

The Menorah, the eight-branched candlestick, was, from the days of Moses, a sign of the presence of God. To this day, it is still associated with synagogue worship and Jewish domestic liturgies. Even now, the Sabbath begins with the kindling of light in every Jewish home, as the mother of the family draws the rays from the flame to her eyes.

History, including archaeology and epigraphy, reveals the significance of light in the temple worship at Jerusalem. Within the Holy of Holies in the Temple, the large central lamp at the altar of incense was surrounded by other lanterns, all of them bent toward the central light. Should the central lamp be extinguished, it might only be relit by fire from the altar itself. In the year 70 C.E., the second temple at Jerusalem was sacked and destroyed during the Jewish-Roman War; to this day in the city of Rome, the Arch of Titus still stands and commemorates in great detail the Roman soldiers carrying off the

Menorah as part of the spoils of war. Today, the Menorah is used as the symbol of the newly reconstituted state of Israel.

The natural image of light in the Hebrew tradition represented Wisdom. Obviously, there is a utilitarian connotation because, after all: "We work while we have the light." However, the most fundamental biblical meaning of light is that of creation and the Creator. The first remembered act of God was to separate the light from the darkness. "And God said: 'Let there be light,' and there was light. *God saw that the light was good*, and He separated the light from the darkness. God called the light 'day,' and the darkness he called 'night.' And there was morning and there was evening, the first day" (Gn 1:3-5).

The general symbolism of light, in all the major religious traditions, equates it with all that is positive in philosophy and worship, including life itself, immortality, and the presence of God.

Light takes precedence in Semitic spirituality because it is the first element of the Creation. It was blessed by God as good, but it is also expressive of the first act of the human mind, since it is the first category to be apprehended. Both knowledge and wisdom are associated with discerning the difference between light and darkness, night and day. A highly intelligent person is, in ordinary speech, said to be "bright."

Twentieth-century archaeologists have discovered symbols of flame and the use of candlesticks in the ruins of first-century Judaism, at the Dead Sea, Qumran, and Masada. They are also present in the remains of the early worship sites. These would have been in existence before the fall of Jerusalem to Titus in 70 C.E. In the fourth century, when the Church at Jerusalem was finally free to practice openly, it borrowed from Jewish traditions of light.

Sometime between the years 381 and 384, a Christian pilgrim named Egeria, probably from Spain, gave evidence in a diary of a unique Jerusalem liturgy. The structure of worship was based upon the extensive use of lamps and candles, which accompanied the chanting of Psalms as part of the daily ritual. At that time, the most prestigious vessel identified among these lights was a burning lantern with Resurrection implications that was carried into the Church buildings from what was the cave of the Lord's tomb. It also recalled the Temple practice of transporting the flame from the altar of incense. In the Christian Jerusalem liturgy, the deacon announced the arrival of the flame: "*Sophia*—Wisdom. The light of Christ illumines all men. Let us attend."

Variations of such practice are recorded in Egyptian, Ethiopian, and Byzantine liturgies, as the Jerusalem usages spread in modified fashion throughout the Christianity of the late Roman Empire.

Light in the Liturgy

IN particular, the Paschal Liturgy, consisting of a night vigil with expressive gestures, underlined the Risen Christ, *Lumen Christi*, and therefore the dawn of a new age. This practice, too, found ready acceptance in Antioch, Ephesus, and Rome itself. An imperial custom of ancient Rome also played a part in the liturgical ceremonies of light. By the third century, Christians closed the day by blessing God with gestures of candles and lamps. The service of Vespers, known as the *Lucernarium*, accompanied by a catechetical instruction, was common among the Christian communities in Carthage, Alexandria, and other Christian centers in Roman-occupied North Africa.

The Canticle of Simeon, derived from the Infancy Narrative of Luke (Lk 2:32), was normally recited at these gatherings: "The Light of Revelation to the Gentiles and the glory of Your People, Israel." Again, reference was made to the presence of God. The identification of Christ with the Light of the Divine Presence was identified with the song of the old priest at the temple: "A light for revelation to the Gentiles, and for the glory of Your people Israel."

The theme of light has been consistent with other references in the Lucan Infancy Narrative. For example, one can find in the song of Zechariah: ". . . tender mercy of our God, by which the rising sun will come to us from heaven to shine on those living in darkness, the shadow of death" (Lk 1:78-79). Accompanied by these words and thoughts was a reiteration of a sense of the presence of God, valid not only for the Jews but also for Gentile Christians.

Luke himself was a Gentile and was careful to emphasize the truth that salvation was also offered to the Gentile believer. This Compline Service is an expression of faith that the Light of God's presence ever was, is now, and will be deep within the shadows of human history. This Light burst forth at the moment of the Resurrection.

The significance of the Jerusalem Paschal candle, the striking of the new fire, and the various practices of the *Lucernarium* found a kind of validation by their adoption into the practices of the Church at Rome. The theme of light, now common among the early Christian communities, became a symbol of hope, of joy, and of prayer. The practice of the temple lamp, the lantern in the Cave of the Tomb, and worship services conducted by candlelight represented a sensibility toward the continuous worship of the court of heaven before the face of God.

During the time of Roman persecutions, lamps decorated the tombs of Christian martyrs. After 312 C.E., when the Edict of Milan granted freedom to Christians, Pope Sylvester II decorated house churches with burning oil lamps, thus designating them as authentic worship sites. With the development of Christian iconography, lamps and candles later adorned altars, images, and statues. In the Middle Ages, they were first placed before the tabernacle of the altar to indicate belief in the true presence of God in the Eucharist.

Even today at Rome, the practice continues. On great feast days, patronal celebrations, or commemorations of the beatification or canonization of some holy person, torches illuminate the entire façade of basilicas, monasteries, and chapels. This remains a source of wonder and delight for the Roman population accustomed, as it is, to live much of its life outdoors.

In his Pontificate, Pope John Paul has contributed to this phenomenon. It was he who introduced the lighted Christmas tree into the Piazza at St. Peter's. For the Jubilee Year, 2000, with the assistance of the Czech hierarchy and government, he arranged a new lighting system for both the façade and the interior of St. Peter's Basilica. That system, so highly technical, is both nuanced and spectacular, and makes this shrine to St. Peter the most beautiful of the churches in the city of Rome.

Another important custom adopted by the Church is taken from the imperial protocol of ancient Roman times. Emperors, members of the royal family, the consuls of Rome, and plenipotentiary ambassadors of the government were escorted on formal occasions by two light-bearing ministers, who served as an escort of honor. Their light was a symbol of reverence, authority, and continuity, for an eternal flame also burned in the imperial quarters of the Palatine Hill; the flame of these candles represented the continuous energy, or dynamic, identified with Rome.

The Churches of Italy, Asia Minor, North Africa, and Gaul adopted the same custom for processions giving two acolytes, or candle-bearers, to the bishop. Later the acolytes were replaced by two deacons. The same significance was implied by this gesture as in civil use, according to the *mores* of the empire. Later, seven-branched candlesticks were set down before the altar, after the Bishop's cortège had proceeded to the sanctuary. The seven-branched candlesticks represented continuity with Hebrew worship, the system of the

Sacraments, and the number seven, which according to biblical numerology represented infinity and the presence of God. Candlesticks appeared on the altar for the celebration of the liturgy as a sign of the presence of God, invoking reverence from the faithful and intending to separate the sacred from the profane.

The same practice occurred in processions of the Gospel. As the Deacon carried the book aloft, he was accompanied by an incense-bearer and two acolytes with candles. This liturgical gesture proclaimed the content of the Gospels as the light of Wisdom, a luminous spirituality, designed to bring comfort from hearing the ways in which God revealed Himself through prophets, patriarchs, evangelists, and sages.

The Concept of Light and the Gospel of the Poor

FROM the eleventh century onward, the laity began to become aware of its own spirituality, encouraged by pastoral and monastic impetus toward reform. This began more than one hundred years before, when in 909 C.E. the Benedictines of Cluny, in Burgundy, sought to restore the simple spirit of their rule. The Benedictine rule itself always treasured the place of Sacred Scripture in the monastic life and gave the prayerful reading of Sacred Scripture a separate classification as a religious devotion called *Lectio Divina*. The tenth and eleventh centuries saw a succession of monastic popes who sought to make the popular life of the Church more pure by exposing the faithful to the reading and teaching of the Bible. They followed the Johannine preface, identifying the "Word" with the "Light."

During this same period, the Papacy became involved in political squabbles with the emperor of Constantinople and the emperor of the Holy Roman Empire. Papal civil servants mingled canonical expressions with biblical references so that the centrality of the Law in the Old Testament was, for example, used to rationalize its Roman centralization.

In the meantime, the people began to look to the Bible for comfort, instruction, and support. Popular religious movements and, with the coming of the friars, itinerant preachers derived great success from propagating the content of the Gospels. The early centuries of the second millennium saw widespread biblical eclecticism, i.e., excluding some ideas and accepting others. The laity enjoyed the biblical presentations, however. These arrived through Mystery plays, translations into the Romance and Germanic languages, and even fictionalized accounts which today would be considered novels.

Monasticism continued to play a great part in illuminating the shadows of the Dark Ages with the light of Scripture. St. Odo, the second abbot of Cluny, drafted, as early as the second decade of the tenth century, an epic poem of biblical inspiration called *Occupatio*. Minstrels carried such lyrics everywhere. By the twelfth century, monastic and lay interest in the Bible was evidenced by a plethora of biblical commentaries. At the same time, St. Bernard of Clairvaux, already cited above, was hard at work structuring a theology of the restoration of the image of God in man. In this, he made widespread use of the Scriptures. He also made rich and numerous references to Mary and Christian devotion to her.

Until the Reformation times, this evangelical movement was simple and straightforward. The Gospels were especially a comfort to the Church of the good, the humble, and the poor. Their messages were, by and large, straightforward; the texts that were used were derived from the dogmatic passages of the Synoptic Gospels of Matthew, Mark, and Luke. The Gospel of John, with its particular theme of Light, really came into its own only at the end of the Middle Ages, when history records the appearance of a wide variety of mystics at the end of the fourteenth century.

From that time forward, the significance of the Johannine *"illumination,"* as an expression of the Mystery of Christ, became a major theme in the history of spirituality, as well as in biblical studies. I personally remember the beginning of my own biblical studies in the seminary, when the professor of hermeneutics offered a series of lectures on the Gospel of John as being the *real* first book of the Bible, first at least in importance. He did this because he said it was the Gospel of Light, which explained the primeval Creation and the new Creation. "In the beginning was the Word, and the Word was with God, and the Word was God. He was with God in the beginning. . . . The Light shines in the darkness, but the darkness has not understood it" (Jn 1:1-2, 5).

Biblical Images of Light

THE Greek word for "light" in the New Testament is *"phōs."* Derived from a verb that means "to shine," it has many usages. Therefore, as a noun, light is no mere passive object. It always conveys the concept of energy. It should be remembered that the Jerusalem houses had no windows; therefore, the several New Testament authors use the word *phōs* in reference to lighting a candle or preparing the wick of an oil lamp. In ordinary language, *phōs* also conveyed the energy of the rays of the sun and the moon.

In Jesus' day and in the time of the primitive Apostolic missions, light was also a metaphorical expression of rhetoric in Hellenic culture and language. It could mean disclosure of a crime, a logical argument toward truth, or some publicity about facts, news, or persons. In the language of the street, one could *"enlighten"* another. Light also was an expression of majesty. It is for this reason that the Apostle Paul and the author of the Book of Revelation used the word *phōs* to describe the splendor around the court of the throne of God (1 Tim 6:16; Rev 21:24). In a way, it is a counterpart to the Mosaic vision of the feet of God, standing on the glowing tiles of sapphire (Ex 24:10).

In the New Testament, use of the word *phōs* is primarily in reference to the person of Jesus. This is especially clear in regard to Jesus' teaching regarding the coming Kingdom of God, and the consequent call to conversion *(metanoia)*. Reference to Jesus as light is made by Paul (Eph 2:17), Peter (2 Pet 1:19), and John

(Jn 3:36; 5:24; 6:40, 47; 11:25-26; 17:3). The authors of these texts borrow directly from Hellenic cosmology which, in either science or poetry, nominated the planet Venus as the "dayspring" or "morning star."

In passing from its lower to higher conjunctions in the sky, Venus appears to the west of the sun at the end of night and announces the coming of day. It rises before the sun. It is the last flash of brilliance in the night. It ushers in the security of the light of day. Authors of New Testament texts and ancient curators of Christian liturgies made this implication in reference to Christ. Besides the Latin ritual, the ancient and primitive faith of early Christians, whether at Jerusalem, Antioch, or Rome, is still found in the chanting of the *Exsultet* before the newly kindled Paschal candle during the celebration of the Easter Vigil.

> May the Morning Star which never sets find this flame still burning: / Christ, that Morning Star who came back from the dead, / and shed his peaceful light on all mankind, / your Son who lives and reigns forever and ever. / Amen.

In the context of the Easter Liturgy, the illumination of Christ implies a certain and secure knowledge about the authenticity of the person of Jesus and the truths he taught by the parables and displayed by the miracles. The Paschal Liturgy presents Him as the harbinger of the already dawning eternal day. The text of the *Exsultet* describes the night as a place of struggle, but the pillar of fire destroys the darkness of sin. The chains of death and the slavery of sin disintegrate when the Light of Christ pierces the darkness. Here the candle is described as "a flame divided but undimmed, a pillar of fire that glows to the honor of God" and "dispels the darkness."

Through faith, "the night [becomes] as clear as day: it [becomes] my life, my joy." The theology of the New Testament borrows from a consistent element as old as Davidic times. The watchman, then, stood on the top tower of Jerusalem to watch for the first sign of the coming day, "the morning star." From this luminous perspective, the evangelists' accounts of the Public Life of Jesus take on new significance.

The evidence of the several New Testament writers is that the word *phōs* was utilized to express the Creator God of Eternity, the new Kingdom of God which is to dawn, and the pledge of God's fulfillment of the Covenant. Most especially, *phōs* refers to the person of Jesus Himself Who is the source of enlightenment and Who enlightens because *He* is light itself.

The poetic reference to Jesus as the *phosphoru,* that is, the "Morning Star," is one of the most primitive liturgical expressions of Christology. According to the *Koine* Greek, in which the books of the New Testament were written, light stands in opposition to *skotos*, i.e., darkness and night, and to *zōphos*, i.e., gloom, bleakness, depression, or hopelessness. New Testament authors, although writing at different times and for different audiences, seemingly conveyed their message in terms of light, as an expression of Christian piety, true knowledge of God, a desire for spiritual things, and imitation of the life of God, Who is love, by imitation of Jesus.

In a word, *phōs* is Wisdom. For example, the mission of Jesus is identified by Matthew 5:14 with the prophetic, liturgical, and wisdom motifs of the Hebrew Scriptures: *"The people who sat in darkness have seen a great light"* (Is 9:2). Deutero-Isaiah proclaimed the mission of the Suffering Servant likewise in terms of light: "After the suffering of His soul, He will see the Light of Life, and be satisfied; by His knowledge My righteous servant will justify many, and He will bear their inequities" (Is 53:11).

The Light of Wisdom likewise inspired this expression from the former rabbinical student, whom we call Paul: *"At one time you were in darkness, but now you are light in the Lord"* (Eph 5:8). Contact with Jesus communicates this light. In the very first New Testament text, Paul refers to his converts as "children of the Light" (1 Thes 5:5). According to Luke and John, the disciples of the Master are "sons of Light" (Lk 16:8; Jn 12:36). Discipleship, of course, implies imitation of the master. Therefore, the author of the First Letter of John makes no hesitation in proclaiming: "He who loves his brother [as Jesus loves] abides in the Light" (1 Jn 2:10).

Light is not stagnant. The Christian vocation is "to go out among others" and not retire into a shell. The Pauline definition of both Christian witness and missionary commitment is summed up in the phrase, *Sensum Christi Habemus* ("We have the mind of Christ") (Phil 2:5). While that passage refers primarily to Christ's humility, it is also expressive of the presence of the Divine, through the demonstration of exquisite tact and quiet confidence. When one assents to the knowledge of being truly filled with the Light of Christ, he or she can go anywhere and associate with anyone without fear of being contaminated.

The missionary quality of the promised Kingdom of God is incited by this maxim from the Sermon on the Mount: *"Let your light shine before men"* (Mt 5:16). The fruit of the imitation of Christ, the Morning Star, and the proclamation of the new Creation, which is the Kingdom of God, is light itself, that is, peace, joy, and trust. When Matthew wrote of "the light that is in you," he used an ordinary candle, lamp, and bowl as the simile for mind, attitude, and conscience as light. Every citizen of Jerusalem would know what he was talking about.

In Jesus' day, housewives used small clay lamps that consumed olive oil drawn up by a flaxen wick. The bowl was also made of clay and held eight quarts of ground cereal. This passage from the Sermon on the Mount is intended to refer even to one's body: "You are the light of the world. A city on a hill cannot be hidden, and neither do people light a lamp and put it under a bowl. Instead they put it on its stand, and it gives light to everyone in the house. In the same way, let your light shine before men, that they may see your good deeds and praise your Father in heaven" (Mt 5:14-16).

To parody the thought of St. Francis de Sales and Cardinal Newman, *lux ad lucem loquitur,* "Light speaks to light." St. Francis and Cardinal Newman chose as mottos, *Cor ad cor loquitur,* "Heart speaks to heart." The Gospel message then is that light speaks to light to the praise of God, Who is light itself. This is also a proverb taken from the frontier Christianity of the nineteenth century, "One kindled spirit enlightens another." If one is devoid of such light, he is either in the shadow of sin or in the effects of sin.

The early Fathers of the Church, namely St. John Chrysostom, St. Ambrose, St. Basil, and St. Jerome, and especially St. Augustine, carried the biblical theme into the ethical sphere. In pastoral sermons, these bishops and doctors spoke of moral, mystical, and spiritual light. They held up the ideals of a *pure conscience,* of blessing each day with moral good- ness; they promised a special inward happiness, which flows from purity of thought, of intention and deed, and a particular consecration to the Gospel. That consecration, no matter from what state of life it is made, is itself holiness or *light.*

Light in the Gospels

IT has been the conventional wisdom that the the- ology of light, or the Luminous Teaching of Jesus, is primarily associated with the Gospel of John. As such it has been the topic of examination by many biblical scholars. However, the subtext of the theme of light is also evidenced in the Letters of Paul, which antedate the composition of any of the Gospels. The same theme is likewise found in abundance in the Synoptic writers, principally in Luke and Matthew.

The Canon of the New Testament places the Gospel of Matthew first in the order of writings, although it may not have been the first composed. Matthew presents the character of Jesus in the role of Rabbi or Spiritual Master. In this capacity, the Jesus of Matthew forms a clear link between the Hebrew Scriptures and the Christian Scriptures. He combines the themes of law from the Old Testament and the Gospel from the New Testament. Matthew validates the prophecies and teachings pertinent to the Mosaic order by demonstration of fulfillment. In Matthew, Jesus' central teaching is clearly the pronouncement of the Kingdom. It is in Matthew that particular properties of the uniqueness of Jesus are identified with the signs of the New Kingdom. These are demonstrated principally through the Beatitudes of the Sermon on the Mount (Mt 5:1-12).

Matthew's Gospel, like that of John, can authentically be said to be a Gospel of the Light. Evidence of the effects of light is found throughout as New Testament witnesses react to disclosures made to them, i.e., amazement, astonishment, surprise. The concept of light in Matthew's Gospel is all about the uncovering of hidden truths which dispels the darkness of ignorance about God's domain, His community, and His plan. Finally, Matthew's Gospel shows a commonsense approach to religion. In the middle of Jesus' Public Life, the Jewish leaders came to Him to be entertained by some sign from heaven.

He replied: "When evening comes, you say,
'It will be fair weather because the sky is red.'
And in the morning, 'It will be stormy because

it is dark and overcast.' You know how to interpret the appearance of the sky, but you cannot interpret the signs of the times. A wicked and adulterous generation looks for a miraculous sign, but none will be given it except the sign of Jonah" (Mt 16:21-24).

The metaphor "sign of Jonah" is a kind of Hebraism, i.e., a particular Jewish literary form which states and reduplicates a proverbial truth. In this case, Jesus is saying that no sign will be given at all. (In the Book of Jonah, the prophet was afraid that the Ninevites would not listen to his preaching; to his amazement they accepted his message *without* any miraculous demonstration.)

Matthew makes it clear that an inner light is necessary to discern the ways of God. The Christian mission involves simple acts of observation and interpretation. Miraculous signs merely delight the senses or shock conventional expectations, but their effect is short-lived. In the above parable, the sky is the cradle of light, and it conveys the significance of the day. The ability to interpret its portents stems from an individual's experience with light. The wicked and adulterous generation lives in darkness, and the proof of their state-of-being is their indiscriminate behavior. Often they are confused because they have learned only to be self-deceptive.

The *Luminous Mysteries of the Rosary* proposed by Pope John Paul II are drawn from such events during the Public Life of Jesus. They flow directly from the Gospels and are concerned with the person of Christ and His mission, especially the inauguration of the Kingdom of God. Each Mystery likewise feeds and enriches the concept of the Christian vocation.

Always a Biblical Foundation

POPE John Paul II has consistently shown, throughout his pontificate, a preference for biblically based devotions. In 1991, while presiding at the Good Friday Stations of the Cross at the Colosseum in Rome, for example, he inaugurated fifteen different Stational events, each of them based on the New Testament. The *Luminous Mysteries of the Rosary* follow this same pattern, with a biblical foundation for every Christic incident chosen. Clearly, his expression of the "Light of Christ" is connected with the image of the Church presented by the Second Vatican Council, *Lumen Gentium,* or "Light of the Peoples." The title *Luminous Mysteries* is also connected with the biblical image of Jesus as "The Dayspring."

The content of His proclamation is the forthcoming Kingdom of Light. Yet while He is the Word, He Himself is also "the Light" (Jn 1:3), and as such He is the promise of that Kingdom which He preaches. Just as the Morning Star anticipates the rising of the Sun and recalls for the believer the renewal of the first morning of Creation, so too does Jesus foreshadow the everlasting promise of the Father that all things will be new: *In principium erat verbum* ("In the beginning was the Word") (Jn 1:1). The juxtaposition of the terms Word, Light, and Beginning by the

Johannine author brings hope for a new beginning with the passing of each day. The concept is not a stranger to our daily language. How often do we hear the term, "I can see light at the end of the tunnel"?

The Christic Connection

ON October 17, 1978, the morning after his election, Pope John Paul II addressed the College of Cardinals who had elected him. They were about to depart the Sistine Chapel, which serves as the Conclave Hall for the designation of a new Pope. He told them that the one event they could anticipate would be his leadership of the Church into the new Millennium, and the celebration of the 2000th anniversary of the Birth of the Messiah. History has witnessed the fulfillment of his prophecy.

In the Apostolic Letter, *Novo Millennio Ineunte* ("On the Threshold of the Third Millennium"), he invited all the People of God to "start afresh from Christ" with the beginning of a new year, a new century, and a new millennium. The Pontiff alluded to this message in *Rosarium Virginis Mariae* (no. 3). The words cited immediately above recall the Bull of Indiction *Incarnationis Mysterium* for the Holy Year of November 29, 1998: "In Jesus Christ the history of salvation finds its culmination and ultimate meaning. In Him we have all received *grace upon grace* (Jn 1:16), having been reconciled with the Father (cf. Rom 5:10; 2 Cor 5:18)."

Besides the prediction of his future Pontifical mission, spoken to the body of prelates who had elected him, the Pope likewise addressed the Christocentric fulcrum of his entire pastoral vision. On March 4, 1979, John Paul II published his first encyclical, *Redemptor Hominis* ("The Redeemer of Man"), in which he clearly stated: "All of us who are Christ's followers must therefore meet and unite around Him" (no. 11).

In the next paragraph, the Pope stated: "Jesus Christ is the stable principle and fixed center of the *mission* that God Himself has entrusted to man. We must all share in this mission and concentrate all of our forces on it, since it is more necessary than ever for modern mankind. If this mission seems to encounter greater opposition nowadays than ever before, this shows that today it is more necessary than ever and, in spite of the opposition, more awaited than ever" (no. 11; *emphasis, mine*).

This was the most synthetic and most comprehensive glimpse into the future agenda of this Pontiff. It is significant that tucked into this prolepsis of his ministry, there is a single quote from the Gospel which identifies his sense of realism: "The children of this world are more astute . . . than the *children of light*." Clearly, this biblical passage had always been a seminal idea in the thought and writing of John Paul II. The concept of light is used now in *Rosarium Virginis Mariae* as an incentive to begin anew. The reference to the "children of light" as being in opposition to the "children of this world" provides a Christic identity for all the members of the Church who "meet and unite around Him."

There is indeed a mission entrusted to Christ, His Church, and each member of the Mystical Body of

Christic. That mission is prayer. All is dependent on God; for that reason, the prayer of the Christian is divided in two parts. One part is worshipful thanksgiving: a gesture of gratitude for Who and What God is, and for the many blessings He bestows. One always begins to pray from the deepest humility before the Majesty and the Benevolence of God-Creator-Father.

The second part of all prayer is a realistic presentation before the Face of God of one's own needs and those of His People. It never need be a source of apology. Dependence on God is a part of life. As, during the Exodus, Moses stood on the hill at Rephidim (Ex 17:8) begging God to show mercy on the Israelites as they experienced defeat from the tribes of Amalek, so every Christian raises heart and hands before the face of the Unseen Father, in union with Christ the Priest, asking that the Almighty One shed mercy and fortitude upon those laboring, suffering, even fighting, to build up the Kingdom on this earth.

It can truly be said of Christ, the Resurrected High Priest in the Court of Heaven, as was said of Moses: He did battle for His people on the hill while they did battle on the plain. Because of the Christians' identity with the Royal Priesthood of Christ through Baptism, this dictum and obligation applies to all the baptized.

In the treasury of the Church's Liturgy and Spirituality, the chanting of the Divine Office has been most closely identified with this prayerful mission of the Messiah. For centuries, the daily prayer of the Breviary has been the obligation of all deacons, priests, and bishops, as well as monks and nuns. The Constitution on the Sacred Liturgy, *Sacrosanctum Concilium*, of December 4, 1963, confirmed this truth. It stated: "The Divine Office is the voice of the Church . . ." (no. 99). It also stated: "The Divine Office, because it is the public prayer of the Church, is a source of piety and a nourishment for personal prayer." This same Apostolic Constitution identified the close place of the Divine Office alongside the daily celebration of the Eucharist.

In the years since the Second Vatican Council, the practice of the Divine Office has been encouraged, and the Breviary has undergone multiple modifications. The past clarification of the Divine Office as a monastic or clerical obligation has given way to a more pastoral application. It would be safe to say that, in the twentieth century, this was largely due to the influence of Dr. Pius Parsh, the Austrian priest who propagated the cause of daily parish celebrations of the Divine Office.

Today, many people, either clerical or lay, carry the Psalms and pray the Divine Office daily, no matter what their station in life. In my own family, one of my cousins, who is a doctor and the father of children, prays the Roman Breviary every day despite a very busy schedule. In the last forty years, the practice has gone from an ecclesiastical obligation, exercised by the few, to a rich, personal religious experience available to the many.

Apparently, the combined participation of clergy and faithful was part of the original schema of the practice of the Divine Office. The earliest fragments of Christian Psalm books and rituals date from sixth-century Rome. At that time, there was no fixed form for celebrating the Breviary. The ritual of each basilica or *titulus*, i.e., a church run by a monastic community or a presbyteral college, varied in length and form.

There is evidence, as noted above, that in some cases all 150 Psalms were recited each day. In other cases, the Psalms were spread out through the week and were accompanied by Scripture readings and Patristic commentaries, principally from Jerome, Ambrose, and Augustine. Universally, the two hours of the change of light, i.e., *Lauds* (morning prayer) and *Vespers* (evening prayer), were designated as the solemn components of the Breviary, since sunrise and sunset demonstrate the presence of God the Creator Who separates light from darkness and darkness from light.

The office was always identified with celebrating God Who is light itself. Over the centuries, attempts were made to stabilize the ritual for universal usage throughout the Latin world. This was especially true at the time of Charlemagne in the ninth century, Pope Gregory VII in the eleventh century, and Pope Pius V in the sixteenth century. Over time, two constants could be identified. One of these was the continuous use of the 150 Psalms as the basis of prayer, especially because that prayer was taken from Scripture, the inspired Word of God, and rendered back to God in His own Spirit-inspired language. The second constant was the quotidian participation in the prayer of Jesus, and mingling that prayer with daily activity to the praise of God, sanctifying the various hours of the day, and pleading for those whose burden it is to toil and suffer in the struggles of the day.

As has been noted from the archaeology of Irish monasticism, at this same time those who did not have access to the texts recited or chanted a series of vocal prayers in order to correspond with the 150 Psalms of the Divine Office. Evidence of the origins of the Rosary is as obscure as that of the Breviary. There is, however, an easily identified parallel between the two. The goals are the same. The theme of light is present. The desire to listen to the Word of God and imitate His Wisdom in Christ is expressed. This is intimacy with God in the Blessed Trinity; contemplation is the fruit of such prayerful activity. Both rituals present the needs of the faithful before the Face of God. With the Apostolic Letter *Rosarium Virginis Mariae,* Pope John Paul II has telescoped all of these elements.

Further, the Pontiff has made an innovation. He has established a permutation consistent with the innovation. His purpose is to convoke a renewed focus on the person of the Christ and His ministry at the dawn of another new millennium. He has broken beyond the number 150, associated with the Psalms. He has filled the long-felt need to identify highlights from the Public Ministry of Jesus, and he has comforted the faithful with the re-presentation of those biblical scenes which shed light. These he has called the *Luminous Mysteries of the Rosary.* It would seem that the gesture of the Pontiff's letter is an affirmation that the Rosary is indeed *a prayer of the Church.*

Part II

The Luminous Mysteries
of Pope John Paul II

Explanatory Note

WHAT follows below is a series of personal meditations upon each of the new *Luminous Mysteries of the Rosary.* They are my personal reflections. Although they draw from Scripture, they do not pretend to be scholarly. Like all prayer, they indicate a certain autobiographical character along with the content.

As a priest of the Passionist Congregation, I have been privileged to be formed, in my seminary days, in a strong biblical tradition. As a result, I have learned the importance of allowing the New Testament texts to speak to me in personal meditation, sermon preparation, or teaching.

It is, I believe, important and useful to follow the method proposed by Pope John Paul II as his own plan for reciting the Rosary: (1) speak the Mystery aloud, (2) choose a Scripture passage and read that aloud as well, and (3) spend a moment or two in silence to compose the scene in the imagination. Finally, pray the decade of the Rosary while allowing oneself to feel the impact of the Mystery's content.

According to the evidence of his writings, Pope John Paul II has observed this practice from his years as a student and laborer in wartime Krakow. The method is as important as the presentation of the New Mysteries.

First Luminous Mystery:
Jesus Is Baptized in the Jordan

THE evidence of the New Testament indicates that this incident in the life of Jesus is unique. This event is recorded in all four Gospels (Mt 3:13-17; Mk 1:9-11; Lk 3:21-22; Jn 1:31-34). As such, it is on a par with the Passion Narratives which appear in every Gospel tradition. The details of this Mystery are recorded by all four evangelists with remarkable similarity.

From the most ancient days of Church life, various Christian liturgical texts in both the East and the West contain evidence that the celebration of the Baptism of Jesus was an ancient and important feast of the Nativity Cycle. Along with the celebration of the Wedding Feast at Cana, the feast of the Baptism of Jesus in the Jordan was connected to the commemoration of the Epiphany, i.e., the presentation of the Child Jesus to the three Wise Men from the East. Evidence of this is still found in the *Magnificat Antiphon* for the second Vespers for the Feast of the Epiphany. It is very ancient.

Three Mysteries mark this Holy Day: Today the star leads the Magi to the Infant Christ; today water is changed into wine for the wedding feast; today Christ wills to be baptized by John in the river Jordan to bring us salvation.

The three events cited are acts of revelation of the divine origin and mission of Jesus. The Magi of the

Epiphany were probably astrologers from present-day Iraq. It must be remembered that there was a Hebrew community still dwelling in the former Kingdom of Babylon. There is evidence that such individuals combined the content of the Bible with Persian cosmology. While the event of the Epiphany is not among the Mysteries of the Rosary, it is important to remember that Christian tradition has always associated that feast with Jesus' Baptism by John and the Wedding Feast of Cana in Galilee.

It is good to remember, too, that the birth of the Messiah was announced to the Gentiles by the light of the star. As we have seen above, the importance of a Morning Star is part of the motif of Light employed by the evangelists and Paul to communicate otherwise ineffable truths about Jesus. It is for this reason that I have chosen the baptismal account of Matthew who likewise narrated the events of the Epiphany to provide the Gospel passage for my reflection upon the Mystery of the Baptism of Jesus in the Jordan.

Then Jesus came from Galilee to the Jordan to be baptized by John. But John tried to deter Him, saying, "I need to be baptized by You, and do You come to me?" Jesus replied, "Let it be so now; it is proper for us to do this to fulfill all righteousness." Then John consented. As soon as Jesus was baptized, He came up out of the water. At that moment, heaven was opened, and He saw the Spirit of God descending like a dove and alighting on Him. And a voice from heaven said: "This is My Son, Whom I love; with Him, I am well pleased" (Mt 3:13-17).

Let us listen again to the title of the Mystery. The words are significant: The Baptism of Jesus in the Jordan. First, let us identify the significance of the phrase "Baptized in the Jordan." In the original Greek accounts, the words used are *"baptizo"* and its adjunct *"eis"* which is a preposition meaning "in," "on," "into," "unto," "for the cause of," "for the sake of."

Let us therefore look at the meaning of the words. Baptizing was a cultic act of purification and consecration for men and women alike, and it is especially evidenced among the various sects of first-century Judaism. From the perspective of the twenty-first century, we are accustomed to looking back to the time of Jesus in order to find a uniform, cohesive expression of the Hebrew faith. But the evidence of the New Testament clearly contravenes this.

Jesus was continually encountering Pharisees, Sadducees, Priests, and Levites in the course of His Public Ministry. They were not a united front against Him. They were not even a united front against each other. The priests of the Temple formed an oligarchy which in part was in league with the Roman occupiers of Palestine. Not only did they supervise the liturgy of the Temple, but they ran the infrastructure of the Jewish civil service, tending even to problems of sanitation, building codes, and water supply. Their main task was to mollify a Jewish population who both religiously and culturally resented the presence of Roman occupiers.

Since the discovery of the Dead Sea Scrolls in 1947, greater attention has been paid to what seemed to be marginal Jewish subcultures. Among these was a quasi-monastic community at Qumran, most probably the center of the Essene Party. Its members were strongly opposed to the contemporary network of the Temple priesthood, considering them to be impure through contact with the hated Gentiles of Rome.

John the Baptist may very well have been representative of such a group, and certainly evidence regarding his prophetic vocation is found both in and outside Scripture. John undertook a mission of reform and repentance in a manner similar to the earlier prophets Isaiah, Ezekiel, and Jeremiah. He foresaw the coming of the new Kingdom, which would be a new Israel. The inauguration of that Kingdom was the work of a long-foreseen Messiah. It was the religious obligation of the current age to prepare the heart for the recognition and the acceptance of God's intervention yet once again in the History of Salvation.

In the Gospel context, Baptism was an act of immersion, of cleansing, and of personal consecration to the content of John's prophetic teaching. In a nation and a culture accustomed to ritual purifications, the significance of Baptism would have been immediately understood. The elements, namely the words, the water, even the passivity of handing oneself over to the action of another, were considered to be a trustworthy act of faith, and therefore led the disciple "into repentance" (Mt 3:11).

Now let us return to the verbal adjunct *"eis."* The first and immediate application of the phrase is that Jesus is baptized into John's mission. As for all of us, Jesus was identifiable by those with whom He associated. The evangelists are unanimous in recording that Jesus' first public encounter was with John the Baptist. Jesus appears unaccompanied to stand on the bank of the Jordan, and then, once He has heard John's explanation of the significance of baptism, Jesus shows that He is convinced. He therefore walks into the river and demonstrates a submission before John. *Jesus chose to be baptized into the mission of John.* He will fulfill it, He will further it, and He will clarify it. This is the first point of understanding to be achieved by reflection upon the Jordan event.

Many things present themselves for reflection upon this point—for example, the relationship with each of the prophets, Jesus' own call to others for conversion, and the parallel consequences of John's mission and that of Jesus. John was clear in that he was merely a prologue to Jesus. But as such, especially through demonstration of his guileless morality, authentic commitment, and naked courage, he was a personal expression of the depth of the radical mission of Jesus.

The encounter of Jesus and John in the Jordan transforms the dynamic of religion for all time. Stories of John and Jesus had already formed part of the Infancy Narrative; their deaths, so heinous, identified the presence of evil in this world. Both were executed by potentates from motives of sheer expediency. In choosing to be baptized into John's mission, Jesus produced evidence that He furthers and deepens the age-old biblical truths which were indicated by the prophets and the sages. Jesus chose to be baptized *in the Jordan.*

In various expressions of the Christian Liturgy, especially in the Church at Jerusalem, the Baptism of Jesus in the Jordan was known as "the Jordan Event." The Jordan River was the principal border of the ancient state of Israel. The Hebrews reached the Promised Land only when they crossed the Jordan under the leadership of Joshua. In the context of the Pentateuch, it was the duplication of the crossing of the Red Sea.

Through the Jordan, the Twelve Tribes emerged into the experience of freedom. From the Red Sea, the Twelve Tribes passed into the land of God, the place of freedom, whereby they might experience the presence of the joy of God through worship and the practice of the Law. Here they were secure. They built a rich culture. Through dramatic figures such as David and Nehemiah, to name but two, the content of the Hebrew Scriptures demonstrates the interaction of God with His family. The land of Canaan, now Israel, circumscribed by the Jordan, was their home.

In reading the Old Testament histories, prophecies and Wisdom passages, as well as praying the Psalms, one becomes used to the majesty and purity of God Who desires intimacy with His people. He is formidable when they set themselves against Him, or, worse, when they neglect Him.

The Old Testament presents God as a *paterfamilias*, i.e., the father of a family, and it is easy to see the reason for which the narratives of the Patriarchs formed the basis of all Hebrew religious writing. Abraham, Isaac, and Jacob, all fathers, are all like God in their own way. There is an absoluteness to their characters, which reflects that in one way or another they have experienced the presence of God. These thoughts are contained in the image of the Jordan as the household walls of God's contact with the lives of men and women. Most of the narratives of the Old Testament are about families.

Again, let us remember to recite the entire title of the Mystery. Therefore the Jordan is recalled by its place as the first public incident in the life of Jesus. As one author has put it, the Cosmic Mysteries begin at the Jordan. What was formally brought into the land across the Jordan is now released back over that frontier into the cosmos. Here is the site of the return of the Voice of God to history, after Sinai.

God announced Himself in and over the River Jordan. His voice moved in two directions—*into* the home of God's Chosen People, and *outward* to the lands of the Gentiles, who are now able to experience the possibilities of likewise entering the presence of God, and, through identity with Christ, to hear and understand the content of the Mystery of being chosen, loved, summoned, and considered a child of God.

The River Jordan likewise recalls the perennial theme of water in the Bible, which includes the waters of Creation, the Great Flood, and the passage through the Red Sea. The use of water is consistent with Hebrew cultic practice and, later, the Christian Liturgy. Moses produced refreshing water before the astonished gaze of a doubting generation (Ex 15:25). The prophets Isaiah and Ezekiel utilized water as a symbol of spiritual revivification and placed its origins in the Temple (Is 55:1; Ez 47:1-6).

The Jesus mandate of the Great Commission to the apostles would couple Baptism with the teaching of all nations: *"Jesus came to them and said, 'All authority in heaven and on earth has been given to Me. Therefore go and make disciples of all nations, baptizing them in the name of the Father, and of the Son, and of the Holy Spirit, and teaching them to obey everything I have commanded you. And surely I am with you always, to the very end of the age' "* (Mt 28:18-20).

In the age of the Christian martyrs, Ignatius of Antioch wrote that the Jordan River's contact with the Lord's physical body brought sanctifying action to the water used in the celebration of the Mystery of Baptism. He implied that water was *now* a sign of Cosmic Redemption. As the primeval symbol of the Creation, water, touched by the Word, i.e., Jesus, highlights the full significance of both the Creation and the Redemption. This symbolism has found expression in almost two thousand years of Easter liturgies, where water used for Baptism is set aside and ritually blessed to indicate the presence of Christ in the actual element of Baptism, water itself.

Let us also recall that the waters of the Jordan were blessed in the crossing of the Twelve Tribes of

Israel, carrying the Ark of the Covenant. The Ark was the vessel of the presence of God in the former dispensation. Now, at the *designated* time, the presence of the entire Trinity comes to rest in, on, and above the Jordan River. Jesus is now the Ark, the new vessel of the presence of God. When the Ark of the Covenant was first carried by the Hebrews in Canaan, it was held high over the water and seemed to float as a new vessel of life, formally symbolized by Noah's Ark. Whereas the Jordan formerly stood as a boundary of protection for the Holy and Beautiful People of God, now it comes to represent the breaking of boundaries. The action of the presence of God flows in all directions and pierces all frontiers. This is the inauguration of another new age, the Kingdom of God. A sense of wonder and continuity rises, for God's possibilities are endless.

The presence of the Trinity over the Jordan is accompanied by the language of the Father: "Here is My Son, My Chosen. I love Him." The words recall the prophet Isaiah:

> Here is My servant whom I uphold, My chosen one in Whom I delight; I will put My spirit on him, and he will bring justice to the nations. He will not shout or cry out or raise his voice in the streets. A bruised reed he will not break, and a smoldering wick he will not snuff out. In faithfulness he will bring forth justice; he will not falter or be discouraged until he establishes justice on earth. In his law, the islands will put their hope. This is what the Lord says—He Who cre-

ated the heavens and stretched them out, Who spread out the earth and all that comes out of it, Who gives breath to its people and life to those who walk on it" (Is 42:1-5).

In the ancient Near East, the term "servant" did not imply some sort of household factotum. Specifically, the word meant a trusted envoy, a confidential representative, an ambassador sent to foreign areas.

In the religious context, such an individual was a prophet. A prophet, unlike a king or priest of ancient Israel, did not receive his office through noble blood. He was identified through another credential. This was always of celestial origin, and it publicly authenticated the prophet's communication by signs and symbols. Clearly, the Jordan-event is also a fulfillment of the Servant prophecy of Isaiah, and the two texts should, in meditation, be juxtaposed and compared.

But now listen, O Jacob, My servant, Israel, whom I have chosen . . . for I will pour water on the thirsty land and streams on the dry ground; I will pour out My Spirit on your offspring, and My blessings on your descendants. They will spring up like grass in the meadow, like poplar trees near flowing streams. One will say, "I belong to the Lord"; another will call himself by the name of Jacob; still another will write on his hand, "The Lord's," and will take the name Israel" (Is 44:1, 3-5).

"A bruised reed he will not break" (Is 42:3).

In His Public Ministry, Jesus will be conscious that He is God's envoy. He will both reveal and demonstrate God's will, but His manner will be both gentle and unobtrusive. "A bruised reed he will not break." The authentication of His prophetic ministry is the theophanous confirmation of the presence of God in the form of the Trinity.

It can be said that Jesus has been baptized into the continuation of John's mission, and thus the mission of all the prophets. He has been baptized in the Jordan, which contains a cosmic significance. Finally, He has been baptized into the role of envoy of God. The characteristics of this last classification had already been foretold by Isaiah. They are gentleness, meekness, and a consecration to fulfill the Will of God. They are also characteristics of the community of God, i.e., the New Kingdom of Israel, which He will inaugurate.

Second Luminous Mystery:
The Wedding Feast at Cana

ON the third day, a wedding took place at Cana in Galilee. And Jesus and His disciples had also been invited to the wedding. When the wine was gone, Jesus' Mother said to Him, "They have no more wine." "Dear Woman, why do you involve Me?" Jesus replied. "My time has not yet come." His Mother said to the servants, "Do whatever He tells you." Nearby stood six stone water jars, the kind used by the Jews for ceremonial washing, each holding from twenty to thirty gallons. Jesus said to the servants, "Fill the jars with water." So they filled them to the brim. Then He told them, "Now draw some out and take it to the Master of the banquet."

They did so, and the Master of the banquet tasted the water that had been turned into wine. He did not realize where it had come from, though the servants who had drawn the water knew. Then he called the bridegroom aside and said, "Everyone brings out the choice wine first, and then the cheaper wine after the guests have had too much to drink; but you have saved the best wine until now." This, the first of His miraculous signs, Jesus performed at Cana in Galilee. He thus revealed His glory, and His disciples put their faith in Him (Jn 2:1-11).

Two very apparent characteristics are carried over from the narrative of Jesus' Baptism in the Jordan. One of these is the use of water, which is so identified with the Creation Narrative, when at first all of the planet was covered with water. The second detail is Jesus' gentleness. The lack of wine at a Jewish wedding was a social embarrassment. Failure to provide proper hospitality on such an occasion was a serious oversight. It was a sign of a Servant, as we have seen according to Isaiah's definitions, that he would be gentle and unruffled. With these thoughts in mind, let us now set the scene.

A few details are known. The wedding took place on a Wednesday, the third day. It was held at Cana, in Galilee. There are two possible sites for this town: a small city about four miles from Nazareth or another site which is about nine miles from Nazareth. This latter place has yet to be excavated. The married couple was obviously close to Jesus' family, and it was important that He and His Mother be there for the celebration. Furthermore, the wedding hall was, at most, a couple of hours walk from Jesus' home. The fact that He was there with His Mother indicates that He had not yet completely withdrawn from His Mother's household.

Most significant of all was the construction of a Roman city known as Sepphoris, only three miles north of Nazareth. This gleaming new metropolis was intended to extend the Roman form of Hellenic culture into Palestine. Instead it produced a backlash in Galilee against Rome. Evidence indicates that Jesus both grew up and functioned as an adult in a time of resurgent Jewish pride which was directed against Rome.

Roman marriages were not permanent, and could easily be dissolved. The evidence of Roman history clearly shows that marriage was a bartering tool among the aristocracy for prestige, power, and pleasure. Roman custom did not guarantee equal partnership between the spouses. The Roman image of marriage and the family was very often a loveless institution.

In the midst of cultural discontent with Roman occupation, the Jews were uncovering again the central traits of their faith. Reference was made to Genesis 1:26-27 whereby the Creator declared that humankind was created in God's image. Humankind consists of a plural composition of male and female, each separately created in God's image, but, when brought together, a direct and multifaceted participation in God's image. The Hebrews saw themselves as furthering the Creation by extending the Family of God through children.

The tenets of the Hebrew Scriptures teach four essential characteristics of marriage. The first is *complementarity*. Marriage forestays the burden of personal loneliness. Man and woman are created to be suitable mutual helpers and therefore complement each other in life's tasks. This clarification of marriage found even in the earliest chapters of Genesis (2:18) would in the New Testament be developed by Paul in the Letter to the Philippians (2:1-11). Complementarity is not a demeaning role. In marriage, the partner enhances the self-image while in the process of helping the other. The fruit is a cohesive human unit of parents and children, which is balanced, harmonious, and unified. In itself, through ordinary daily function, the family is a prayer praising God by mirroring back to Him His own image.

The second hallmark of marriage, according to biblical custom, is its *permanency*. Genesis 2:24 speaks of "cleaving." The marriage bond is permanent. God's ideal for marriage is that it be exclusive. Practices of easy separation or divorce were pagan and therefore sinful, for they were devoid of faith.

Faith, after all, is not an assent to the truths of a creed, but rather is about being *faithful*. Again, this is an image of God. His fidelity to His people constitutes the evidence of the whole of the Hebrew Scriptures. The obvious example is the covenant of Sinai itself and the exchange between God and David regarding the construction of the temple. God's fidelity also is demonstrated through the prophets, who continually remind the Israelites that He will reconstitute His people.

The third characteristic is the *unity* of marriage. Again, we find this evidence in the Book of Genesis (2:24) which calls for the coupling of man and woman in "one flesh." Roman practices offended Jewish sensibilities in Jesus' day. Homosexuality, incest, adultery, and, most especially, cultic prostitution were not only intolerable but a source of alienation between the Jews and Romans. Such sexual practices were merely for gratification and were validated only by tales of mythic gods from pagan courts and temples. The central tenet of the Jewish faith was embedded in the marriage ritual: God is One. There were no other gods and no other codes of morality which could legitimately contravene the exercise of discretion in sexual behavior.

Finally, *intimacy* is the most consoling fruit of Jewish marriage. Exclusivity and closeness guarantee this consolation. Jewish law clearly delineates times for both the practice of sexual relations and the temporal abstinence from sexual relations. Mutual consent is always required. No spouse shall exploit the other sexually. Mutual delight in companionship is the recognition of the Jewish Sages (Prov 5:15-19 and Eccl 9:9). The entire Book of the Song of Songs freely borrows from the wedding experience to poetically portray the loveliness of God's commitment to His people. In contrast, the prophets did not hesitate to draw on marital tragedy to describe sin and the nation's fracture of a covenant commitment. They likened such action to adultery and prostitution.

Given the times and the occupation of Palestine by Rome, the presence of Jesus at the wedding at Cana clarifies the significance of marriage as it has been treasured by the evidence of the Old Testament. Marriage is not only about the individuals who are espoused; it is also about God and the aura of holiness, purity, and light which surrounds Him. To this day, the lighting of the Menorah, by the wife and mother of the family on the eve of the Sabbath, recalls the metaphysical presence of God within the holy institution of marriage and the continuity of the family (human life) through the ages.

The presence of Jesus is accompanied by a sign, which is not a dramatic wonder but rather an act of discretion, expressive of Jesus' concern for the reputation of the newlyweds, a sensitivity that He shared with His Mother. The language *archēn tōne sēmeiōn* ("beginning of signs") is the characteristic of the Evangelist John's thematic presentation of his Gospel (Jn 2:11). Signs are important in the action. Their significance, however, is found in what they contain. In this case, the elements of the miracle convey the message of the event.

Having been bidden by His Mother, Mary, Jesus requests the steward to have his footmen fill six large, heavy containers with water. In fact, it is an ugly task. The containers are cold, hard, and heavy. With water added, they are all the heavier. While water is precious in the Middle East, it is ordinary and flat-tasting. The gesture of the steward in tasting the wine is actually the evidence of the miracle. There is no special wording or gesture from Jesus. Suddenly, what was formerly both ordinary and cumbersome had been transformed not only into another substance but also into what was both delicious and a cause of wonderment to the witnesses and the partygoers.

Herein lies the importance of the miracle for the whole Church. The daily actions of human life are often cumbersome and pedestrian; however, when this world is seen as a vessel of the dawning Kingdom of God, what is ordinary suddenly takes on the finest delicacy of the human palate, and one is able to be enriched by the sense of the presence of God.

In light of the above, this miracle makes perfect sense when seen against the theology of marriage as outlined in the Hebrew tradition from the Book of Genesis. The situation of the city of Sepphoris, as a Roman enclave in the territory of pious Judaism, threatened to affect the mores of that piety. The presence of Jesus confirms continuity with the traditional Jewish theology of marriage and its emphasis on the image of God in the mutual love of two persons. Highly significant for everyone, however, is the fact that, in Christ, God is at work in the ordinary. In Christ, He transforms whatever is hard, heavy, and cold into a container of delicacies yet unimagined by human expectation.

Third Luminous Mystery:
The Proclamation of the Kingdom of God

After John was put in prison Jesus went into Galilee, proclaiming the Good News (*euaggelion*—gospel) of God. "The time has come," He said. "The Kingdom of God is near. Repent and believe the Good News" (Mk 1:14).

In the second *Luminous Mystery*, the Wedding Feast at Cana, Jesus addressed His Mother: *"Dear Woman . . . My time has not yet come"* (Jn 2:4). The pattern of the Johannine Gospel pictures Jesus as moving, from that moment, inevitably, toward His final destiny. Jesus' destiny is recorded by John in the second half of his Gospel (Jn 13—21), and embraces His Betrayal, Arrest, Condemnation, Passion, Crucifixion, and Death, and finally His Glorious Resurrection. In the Synoptic Gospels, on the other hand, the movement toward that destiny is demonstrated in the Public Life of Jesus through a unique ministry. Jesus is forming a People who are to be the repository of His revelation and the beneficiaries of His grace.

The Public Life of Jesus, thus focused on the coming *basileia* (Kingdom), is perhaps the richest decade of the whole Rosary since so much biblical material is at its disposal. The Mystery of the

Proclamation of the Kingdom of God requires careful reflection, meditation, and attention. The central theme of this Mystery explicitates the love of Christ for His Church. Yet, paradoxically, during the Public Life of Jesus, the Church was not yet a reality.

In the encyclical *Mystici Corporis* ("The Mystical Body") of 1943, Pope Pius XII had this to say: "It is impossible to name a moment in the Life of our Redeemer when He did not labor for the formation or consolidation of His Church (no. 111)." The entire life and mission of Christ was centered in the Church. During His Public Life, Jesus was engaged in the work of forming the New People of God. He did this by demonstrating the truths of the Kingdom, i.e., through His parables, through His miracles, through His sermons (most notably the Sermon on the Mount), and through His call.

In summoning first the apostles and the disciples, God was again laying the foundation for a covenant of loving kindness (*hesed*—love). Through a recall of the life of Moses one sees the parallel. Moses was the instrument of the formation of Israel as the People of God in the darkness of pagan Egypt. He validated his mission with a multiplicity of miracles and oracles. The words of Moses, whether before Pharaoh or even the Hebrews, were met with doubt and resistance.

In the days of Jesus, His many explanations of His own person and His mission met with suspicion and cynicism from the Jewish leadership. As if in a drama, the characters of the Pharisees, the priestly Sadducees, the Levites, and the Scribes are all important. They are repetitious figures as if from the time of Moses. They supplied an endless chain of foils for the narrative.

The Sermon on the Mount (Mt 5—7) actually duplicates the Mosaic motif. It is a masterpiece of staging. Moses brought the tablets of stone down from Mount Sinai. These were the rules to be enjoined on God's Chosen People in the Promised Land. Now, within that very Promised Land, Jesus presents ten new precepts, e.g., "Blessed are the poor in spirit, for theirs is the *Kingdom of Heaven*" (Mt 5:3). In the account of the Sermon on the Mount, the elements of the formation of the People of God are present. Jesus observes the crowds. Among them are disciples, a term defined as "those who learn." The Commandments of Sinai are prescriptive. All begin with the words, "Thou shalt . . ." or "Thou shalt not . . . ."

The Beatitudes, instead, commence with the unusual invitation, *Makarioi*, i.e., "Blessed." The original text of the first Beatitude reads *"autōn estin ē basileia tōne ouranōn"* ("Of them is the kingdom of the heavens") (Mt 5:2). The lesson here is that the New Kingdom of God is attitudinal; the practice of deeds, the observance of rituals, and the concern for purifications or ceremony are secondary. Jesus' teaching invites high moral inclination and commitment.

Over the centuries, both the Kingdom of God and the Sermon on the Mount have frequently been dismissed as being totally unrealistic. The lesson of history is that every age is given to prioritizing materialism or quest for power. The Christian is detached. Within the People of God, the pilgrim is *proud* to function with a dependence on God. Poverty of Spirit stands over and against the proud, the self-sufficient, the prestigious, and the acquirer of possessions.

Members of the Kingdom of God receive an immediate reward. They are called *Makarioi*, "Blessed." In Jesus' times, that word "happy" expressed conviviality. Examples are delight in a child, the fulfillment of one's hopes or expectations, family celebrations such as bar mitzvahs, weddings, and religious festivals. The blessedness of the Kingdom conveys an ultimate sense of well-being, distinctive spiritual joy, inner serenity, and gratitude for having been favored and chosen. It recalls the phrase *makariousin me* ("me blessed") of Mary's *Magnificat* (Lk 1:48): "*He has looked upon the humiliation of the handmaid of Him. Understand this, from now on all the generations will deem me blessed.*" (This rendition is a transliteration of the Greek.)

The parallel use of the word applies now not only to Mary, as the Mother of God, but to the apostles, and to the Church, which will bring forth Christ from generation to generation. The bliss of the Kingdom of God is not something that is earned; joy is a recompense for those who believe the Kingdom, see the Kingdom, and adhere to the Kingdom. As at Sinai, God is the dynamic of the New People of God, the Kingdom of Heaven. The core truth is that of the Sovereignty of God. Any individual who kneels before the presence of God need not fear to stand before any man.

A student is not above his teacher, nor a servant above his master. It is enough for the student to be like his teacher, and the servant like his master. If the head of the house has been called Beelzebub, how much more the members of his household! *So do not be afraid of them.* There is nothing concealed that will not be disclosed or hidden that will not be made known (Mt 10:23-26).

While reiterating Moses' claim regarding the strength and sovereignty of God, Jesus demonstrates the content of His message by simple, ordinary gestures. Moses emerged from the theophany of Sinai with the tablets of stone. "Mount Sinai was covered with smoke because the LORD descended upon it in a fire. The smoke billowed up from it like the smoke from a furnace, the whole mountain trembled violently, and the sound of the trumpet grew louder and louder. Moses spoke and the voice of God answered him" (Ex 19:18-19). The theophany of God was an impressive display of meteorological sights. By contrast, Jesus merely sits on the mountain. This is a paradoxical gesture containing two implications.

First, sitting down is the traditional rabbinical position for explaining the Law. Secondly, sitting indicates also the domestic welcome to be "among" and "of" the people. The rabbinic ideal has remained the same. Neither of royal nor of priestly blood, the teachers of Jewish spirituality did not separate themselves from the population by regalia. The ideal of the

Pharisees, for example, was to be of service to the people, to be an example for the people, and to instruct the people. The ideal of Jesus was like theirs; what is in the heart is demonstrated by the deed. By sitting on the mountain, Jesus was repeating the domestic gesture of a rabbi, sharing His own inner life and personal mission within His household.

Those who would accept His teaching were already participating in His destiny. The teaching "Blessed are those who are persecuted because of righteousness, for theirs is the *Kingdom of Heaven*" (Mt 5:10) is Jesus' personal identification with those who are misunderstood because of their piety, meekness, and purity of heart. It recognizes the idolater as one who is preoccupied with wealth, prestige, and power, and who does not hesitate to use and abuse another to gain an ephemeral reward. The victim of misuse of authority already possesses the Kingdom of Heaven. Every truth listed in the Beatitudes would be perfectly demonstrated by Jesus in the four accounts of His Passion Narrative.

In particular, Matthew had arranged the material of his Gospel to highlight the concept of the Kingdom of God in Jewish terms. In the preceding section, Jesus inaugurated His preaching in the town of Capernaum. This was the site of Peter's house, and Jesus made it His first base of operations. From there He went to the synagogue, i.e., the traditional *schul* of the Rabbi, to declare Himself. He *is* the fulfillment of the prophecy of Isaiah:

"The people living in darkness have seen a *great light*; on those living in the land of the shadow of death, *a light has dawned*" (Is 9:2).

The New Kingdom is inaugurated through the fulfillment of the prophecies. Once the disclosure of His identity, "Messiah," was proclaimed, the challenge of Jesus' preaching of *metanoia* ("change yourself completely") became the consistent theme of everything He has to say: "Repent, for the Kingdom of Heaven is near" (Mt 4:17). Put another way, the Proclamation of the Kingdom declares: *"You are under the specter of the presence of God."*

The Proclamation is followed by the Call. At the lakeside of Galilee, Jesus greeted Simon Peter and his brother Andrew with the words, *Deute opisō mou*, "Come after Me" (Mt 4:19). Next, these words were repeated to the sons of Zebedee, James and John, who were engaged in their labor. Both sets of brothers were fishermen, obviously in family businesses. The Call shatters business attitudes and family preoccupations. More importantly, God's business is always deemed *urgent* by this demonstration, transcending even natural concerns for household and livelihood.

Immediately prior to the account of the Beatitudes, Matthew narrates that Jesus was reported around the countryside to be some sort of miracle-worker. He was a healer of every kind of disease, either physical, mental, inherited, or accidental. In those days illness was identified with demonic-possession. Superstition and witchcraft were not unknown even among God-fearing Jews. Jesus' mission had not yet brought Him to Jerusalem. Yet His fame spread there as well as to the cluster of Roman towns along the Mediterranean known as the Decapolis. These were noted for their sophisticated Greek culture and their emphasis on science. Even their citizens were interested in Jesus.

Syria was the de facto Roman capital of the province, which included Palestine. News of Syrian interest in Jesus prefigured Jesus' implications for Rome and the whole world. The means of communication were already implied. Colonies of Jews, clustered around their synagogues, did daily business with Arabs and Romans in Syria. For business and religious purposes, they networked with other Jewish colonies, and the word about Jesus spread rapidly. Naturally, miracles caught everyone's immediate attention.

Miracles of healing were of particular importance as the prologue to the Proclamation of the Kingdom of God and the revelation of those precepts (Beatitudes) which comprise its Constitution. Jesus made every effort neither to bask in the title "miracle-worker" nor to identify Himself solely with that power, yet it was to little effect: "Wherever He went—into villages, towns, or countryside—they placed the sick in the marketplaces. They begged Him to let them touch even the edge of His cloak, and all who touched Him were healed" (Mk 6:56).

The miraculous deeds of Jesus are specifically intended to illustrate the content of His teaching: "When the Sabbath came, He began to teach in the synagogue, and many who heard Him were amazed.

'Where did this man get these things?' they asked. 'What is this wisdom that has been given Him, that He even does miracles' "(Mk 6:2)? Even from the very beginning of His Public Ministry, the common-sense response of Jesus' first audience linked the wonders He performed with the wisdom about the Kingdom which He sought to disseminate.

The Johannine Tradition clarifies Jesus' vocation through the narrative of the first half of the Gospel (Jn 1:19—12:50). Scholars have come to label this section of John's Gospel as the Book of Signs, whereby Jesus' miracles occasioned prolonged discourses about the significance of God's mercy. The tangibility of *hesed* ("mercy") is exemplified by healing. John's Gospel demonstrates a healing ministry and mission for the future Church and its members. On a deeper level, they represent the infinite benefits of "covenantal grace."

The Johannine miracles are about compassion. They arise out of the movement of Jesus' heart. Among them are the restoration to health of the official's son at Capernaum (Jn 4:46-54), the healing of the sick man beside the pool at Bethesda (Jn 5:1-9), the cure of the man born blind (Jn 9:1-7), and the raising of Lazarus from the dead (Jn 11:1-44). All of these occasions show an emotional side to Jesus. He is moved by the plight of the poor. At the same time, they demonstrate restoration and reconstitution. This is also the attitude of God the Father.

Other miracles show Jesus' power over nature. Yet, they also disclose the inner sentiment of Jesus. They are expressions of Jesus' delicacy toward other human beings: the feeding of the five thousand (Jn 6:6-13), the walking on the water as a comfort to the disciples (Jn 6:19-21), the Resurrection account of feeding the apostles with a large catch of fish (Jn 21:1-11), and, of course, the miracle of the water turned into wine (Jn 2:1-11). This wonder again contains the elements of paradox. It comes about as the result of an ordinary family exchange between mother and son. Jesus' intention is to prohibit embarrassment for the new bride and groom. Except for immediate observers, seemingly the event hardly merits notice.

The signs are accompanied by a Rabbinic form of teaching. They portend the Glory of God already in Jesus. They are recorded in all four Gospels, and the attitude of Jesus is not a demonstration of false modesty. Instead, the Sovereignty of God is proclaimed. For God is the author of wonders. Jesus' humility is to be imitated by the New People of God. Jesus' summation of His actions and His words is synthesized by Matthew: "Go and learn what this means, 'I desire mercy [hesed] and not sacrifice'" (Mt 9:13).

Jesus' miracles and His teaching are best understood by contemplation of His mode of approach and His gentle and simple manner. Against a background of invective from the religious oligarchy of first-century Judaism, and even the ascetic way of John the Baptist (Mt 11:18-19), the way of Jesus is simple, gentle, and all-embracing.

All the Gospel accounts of Jesus' miracles are intended to shed light. That light is definable in the concept of hesed, that Hebrew word, so prevalent in the prophets, that transcends an easy apprehension of God. It has been perennially grasped by the image of unqualified love between mother and child. The manner of Jesus' healing, His sermons, and His sayings *is* the content of the Gospel. Jesus' approach is generous, gratuitous, forgiving, simple, uncategorical, and at-the-ready.

Jesus pierced attitudes that were still prevalent in first-century Palestinian society. The discovery of the Dead Sea Scrolls in 1947 evidenced widespread attitudes of prejudice, bias, and intolerance. The existence of the Hasidim (people of covenantal grace or mercy— *hesed*) affirms that the Judaism of the day was neither harmonious, nor homogeneous, nor cohesive.

Against the background of Roman-occupied Palestine, the theme of *universalism* would have stood out in Jesus' explanations about the Kingdom. Reconciliation is the standard of the New People of God and, therefore, of the Kingdom of God. It was Jesus' intention to bridge the public gulf between Jew and Gentile. Jesus is the heir to the prophet Isaiah: *"The nations will see your* [i.e., Jerusalem's] *righteousness and all kings your glory; you will be called by a new name that the mouth of the Lord will bestow. You will be a crown of splendor in the Lord's hand, a royal diadem in the hand of your God"* (Is 62:2-3). How is this to be accomplished? The answer is the recognition that conscience calls to conscience!

Jesus' many encounters uncover blunt hearts, obscurantism, complexity, and the tenacious adherence to arbitrary standards. Jesus' principle of universalism finds its moral corollary: *"Judge not, lest you be judged"* (Mt 7:1). To understand Jesus, one must imitate Him. Such behavior requires total generosity and absolute simplicity. Jesus' advice to the rich young man does not disparage wealth. Instead, it is about purity of heart, totality of consecration, and a realistic assessment of the purpose of life and its responsibilities. The Kingdom of God is based upon truth which otherwise can be masked by worry for and love of this world's goods and promises.

In light of that truth, Jesus' message makes perfect sense: *"Go, sell all that you have and distribute it to the poor"* (Mt 19:21). The gift of the Kingdom was denied the rich young man, who went away sad because he had great wealth. Righteousness by works, or the acquiring of education, prestige, or power, or even undertaking pious practices is simply not possible. God alone is good (Mt 19:17). This clarifies the meaning of the Kingdom. To enter life fully is to be near God.

Miracles are one form of demonstration of the significance of the Kingdom of God. They indicate through Jesus' sensitivity to pain that the God of Sinai is a loving Father. They must be seen alongside the Gospel story-parables. To understand Jesus' proclamation of the Kingdom, one should pay careful attention to them. They indicate a culture of communication and teaching among first-century Jews. Jesus did not originate the use of parables; they were frequently used by other itinerant rabbis and were usually homey, rural, and ironic.

An excellent Gospel example is the story of Lazarus and Dives (Lk 16:19-31). The popular imagination has consistently identified Lazarus, the poor man, as the hero. In fact, Lazarus is the foil. Dives, the anti-hero, is the subject of the message. Jesus, the narrator, displays His sense of irony here. Lazarus did not go to heaven because he was poor. Dives did not go to hell because he was rich. His soul was condemned *because he had so hardened his heart* that he never perceived simple humanity. Only after his death and condemnation did he appreciate the importance and beauty of a single drop of water.

A similar parable is that of the Prodigal Son. While forgiveness is the obvious leitmotif, the central character is neither of the two sons. Instead, it is the loving, patient, and understanding father. *He* represents God. The Prodigal Son signifies impetuous youth. The conventional wisdom of the Jewish sages is: "One cannot unring a bell," yet the mercy sought by the Prodigal Son was granted to him because he ultimately achieved honesty, repentance, and the confession of his guilt. The elder brother, however, despite his upstanding ways, consistency, and responsibility, housed in his chest an ugly heart. He is jealous, resistant, and mean of spirit. Yet the father is willing to accept and embrace both of them. *His* love is endless.

This is the God of the New Testament. Mercy and kindness are His way. Jesus recommends imitation of the Father in order to enkindle the spirit of the Kingdom: "But I tell you who hear Me: Love your enemies, do good to those who hate you, bless those who

curse you, pray for those who mistreat you. If someone strikes you on one cheek, turn to him the other
also. If someone takes your cloak, do not stop him
from taking your tunic. Give to everyone who asks
you, and if anyone takes what belongs to you, do not
demand it back. Do to others as you would have them
do to you" (Lk 6:27-31).

Whether the Kingdom of God is phrased in terms
of the miracles, the parables, or the sermons, it is
done so with quintessential simplicity, which may be
summed up: "Love one another, because, as you well
know in your hearts, love is good, and because God
loves you." That message was rejected by the high-
ranking cliques, cabals, and oligarchies in the first
century. Jesus' teaching was resisted because it contained a universal appeal and was not oriented
toward the organization of, or support for, another
kind of Hebrew elite.

Jesus was opposed also because of the *manner*
with which He addressed the crowds. The Scribes,
Pharisees, and Priests resented His kindness, His simplicity, and, consequently, His popularity. It is a fact
that Jesus' special universal appeal provoked the envy
of the Quisling Temple staff. *They* plotted to kill Him.

Jesus spoke with authority. Naturally, this too
provoked ill feeling. His adversaries used arbitrary
conventions as credentials for their message and
directives. Clearly, they also operated out of motives
of expediency. Jesus, on the other hand, spoke with
the authority of God, Whom he dared to call *Father.*
Obviously, no one else in the Hebrew tradition would

presume to pierce the veil of the Sovereign God of Sinai with the use of such familial terms. But for Jesus, God was *Abba*. Jesus communed with God through solitude, silence, and reflection, and not primarily through the prescriptions of temple and synagogue. He therefore offered a spirituality, as distinct from religious discipline. Jesus' very presence provoked envy, gossip, and avarice. When taken together, these represent the "kingdom of darkness."

The experience of the ages since the time of Christ has come to identify the difference between sin and beauty. The Fathers of the Church and the Saints of the Christian era have spoken together or separately about a choice which must be made, once the Kingdom of God has been grasped as a concept. *Is love at the heart of things or is wickedness at the heart of things?* In either case, it is a matter of the ordinary virtues of ordinary people, or the ordinary sins of ordinary people. Few are called to heroic deeds. Few enter into dramatic crimes. *All* are called to make the choice as to which kingdom they will enter.

In the days of the Second Vatican Council (1962-1965), the participants continually repeated the Council's seminal theme: "*Christus Propter Ecclesiam Venit*," which translates, "Christ came because of the Church." The supreme act of God's love, expressed by Christ's Passion, lies at the foundation of the Church, but its constitution is patently the formation of the New People of God by the proclamation of the Kingdom of God. The importance of the Kingdom of God is illustrated by its consistent demonstration by all the evangelists who used several literary tools to demonstrate its meaning.

More than any other Mystery of the Rosary, this third Luminous Mystery offers the greatest amount of biblical material for reflection and meditation. Because it is at the heart of the Gospels, this biblical Mystery can provide much opportunity for moments of personal prayer and reflection.

Fourth Luminous Mystery: The Transfiguration of Jesus on Mount Tabor

AFTER six days, Jesus took Peter, James, and John with Him and led them up a high mountain, where they were all alone. There He was transfigured before them. His clothes became dazzlingly white, whiter than anyone in the world could bleach them. And there appeared before them Elijah and Moses who were talking with Jesus. Peter said to Jesus, "Rabbi, it is good for us to be here. Let us put up three shelters—one for You, one for Moses, and one for Elijah." He did not know what to say; they were so frightened. Then a cloud appeared and enveloped them, and a voice came from the cloud: "This is My Son, Whom I love. Listen to Him!" Suddenly, when they looked around, they no longer saw anyone with them except Jesus.

As they were coming down the mountain, Jesus gave them orders not to tell anyone what they had seen until the Son of Man had risen from the dead. They kept the matter to themselves, discussing what "rising from the dead" meant (Mk 9:2-13).

The Feast of the Transfiguration of Jesus (August 6) holds special meaning for Pope John Paul II. It is the anniversary date of the death of his papal predecessor, Pope Paul VI, to whom he was particularly close. Pope Paul was aware, by the evening of that day in 1978, that he was in *extremis*. Among his last words, he told his household: "On this, the great Feast of the Transfiguration, I want to recite the Angelus for all the faithful of the Church." The dying Pontiff was also conscious of the fact that he was not in Rome, but at Castel Gandolfo. As he was dying, he was mindful of the feast day.

Pope Paul VI was always conscious of the personal significance of a spirituality of the Transfiguration, and he recorded it:

The Father sends His Son, the Son Who represents God's mercy, Who translates it into an act of love toward me, an act of complete self-abandonment to the Father, because He must save me too, as destitute as I am. But a special grace is needed for this, the grace of Conversion. I have to recognize God the Father's action in the Son in *my* regard. Once I acknowledge that, God can work in me through His Son: He gives me grace, the grace of Baptism. After the grace of being reborn to God's life, my life becomes a tension of love with God drawing me toward Himself. And the loving hand of God draws me onward toward His mercy, which raises me up when I fall; I have to fix my gaze on Him to be drawn upward, yet again *(emphasis, mine)*.

In the early days of his pontificate, Pope John Paul II thoroughly familiarized himself with the spirituality of his predecessor by reading over personal notes and journals, as well as by engaging in long conversations with the surviving priest-secretaries. Against this content of Pope Paul VI's journal, as cited above, the advice from *Rosarium Virginis Mariae* regarding the Transfiguration makes clear and perfect sense:

"The Mystery of Light par excellence is the Transfiguration, traditionally believed to have taken place on Mount Tabor. The glory of the Godhead shines forth from the face of Christ as the Father commands the astonished Apostles to 'listen to Him' (cf. Lk 9:35 and the parallels) and to prepare to experience with Him the agony of the Passion, so as to come with Him to the joy of the Resurrection and a life transfigured by the Holy Spirit" (RVM, no. 21).

This Mystery pivots upon an event recorded not only by Mark but also by Matthew (17:1-13) and Luke (9:28). Yet the *most* significant parallel is found in the Petrine Tradition of the New Testament: "For He received honor and glory from God the Father, when the voice came to Him from the Majestic Glory saying, 'This is My Son, Whom I love; with Him I am well pleased.' We ourselves heard this voice that came from heaven when we were with Him on the sacred mountain" (2 Pt 1:17-18).

The inclusion of the Mystery of the Transfiguration in the devotion of the Rosary is a clear indication of the Pope's piety. Seen against the reflections of his predecessor, Pope Paul VI, he is conscious of a certain spiritual continuity. Among other things, Pope John Paul II is conscious that he stands in the Petrine Tradition of the Church's witness to Christ. Highlighting *this final theophanous intervention* before Jesus embraced His death, in obedience to the Father, the Pontiff has identified the Transfiguration as *the* Luminous Mystery of the Rosary. Why? Part of the answer lies in the evidence of Scripture, while the other part has to do with Christian anthropology, i.e., human nature as redeemed by grace.

The consistency of the evangelists tells us much. All three Synoptics, in substance, recorded that the Transfiguration occurred "six days later" (Mk 9:2, Lk 9:28, Mt 17:1). But six days after what? The incident recorded as occurring immediately before is an encounter between Peter and Jesus. Hard sayings were put to Peter by Jesus. Jesus revealed the unalterable components of faith in Him, as will occur again many times throughout Jesus' adult life. Peter's faith in Jesus would be put to the test.

The confession of Christ would never be easy for Peter, as was demonstrated best by the Denial Scene (Mk 14:66-72). Luke, writing of that occasion, even demonstrated through the poetry of his phrasing that Peter could be a fit candidate for Lucifer: "Simon, Simon, Satan has asked to sift you as wheat" (Lk 22:31). The "S" sound, pronounced in the first letter of the opening three words of that passage in Greek, was deliberately intended by the author of that Gospel to convey the hissing of the serpent.

All the apostles demonstrated their discipleship, their openness to Jesus, and their adherence to Jesus. To their own amazement, however, their behavior was often weak and cowardly. Jesus displayed a special bond of intimacy with Peter, James, and John, although they were quite like their confreres. The event of the Transfiguration, as recorded in the New Testament by Peter, Matthew, Mark, and Luke, addressed the issue of inadequate faith.

In the New Testament texts, Exodus images of Sinai are recalled by this event. In Matthew and Mark, not only does this show consistency with the Baptismal Narrative, as it were, a developing Christology, but it also serves as an affirmation of Jesus' divine origin. The period of "six days" parallels the time of the cloud-cover of God over the great mountain during the period of the Exodus. The Lord said to Moses, "I am going to come to you in a dense cloud, so that the people will hear me speaking with you and will always put their trust in you" (Ex 19:9). This passage should be juxtaposed with another: "For six days, the cloud covered the mountain, and on the seventh day, the Lord called to Moses from the cloud" (Ex. 24:16).

In the Tabor event, the chosen apostles represent the Twelve Tribes of old. Peter, James, and John collectively represent the future Church. The Tabor Event was clearly for their benefit. The Transfiguration is an expression of God's understanding of and love for His Church: *"Deus dilexit ecclesiam."* In the Old Dispensation, one man, Moses, was the receptacle of the Revelation of God; in the New Dispensation, the company *(koinonia)* of the three will, in accepting Christ, become together the vessel of reception of Divine Revelation in history. They represent the College of the Apostles and the Church, even to the present day.

Depending on the Gospel narrative in which they are found, apparitions signify the deference of previous religion to the person of Christ. *He* is the focal point of that theophany, i.e., physical signs and wonders associated with manifestations of the presence of God, e.g., earthquake, thunder, and lightning. The figure of Moses summarizes the Covenant of Sinai, which is the formation of the family of God out of the Twelve Tribes, and the pledge of salvation and protection. The figure of Elijah evokes his particular role among the prophets, i.e., to announce the restoration of the holiness of Israel (2 Kgs 2:11). Elijah was that prophet whose holiness was previously unparalleled in all of human history, so much so that he did not even die, but was transported to heaven by a fiery chariot. In these two figures, Holiness itself, and the sacred traditions of the Lord, *Adonai*, bend in reverence to Jesus.

The Father's words take on new significance. In a manner already demonstrated at Jesus' Baptism in the Jordan, although not before an audience of these three, Jesus' nature was identified by the voice of the Father: "This is My Son Whom I love. Listen to Him" (Mk 9:7). God's voice now certainly again identified Jesus as God's own intervention in human history for the sake of its salvation. God's love for His Son can be authenticated by no greater witness than that of His own voice.

The Synoptic Gospels pointedly position this passage among other texts. The evangelists repeat, almost verbatim, the identifying words of the Father in such a manner as to delineate the urgency and inevitability of Jesus' mission. Jesus is, by His own prediction, destined to be arrested, degraded and soon put to death. The final point of the Father's pronouncement, *"akoūete autou,"* "Listen to Him" (Mk 9:7), charges the nascent Church with its future and constant mission. The verb is listed in the imperative tense. Listening now is not about instruction, as previously viewed at the inauguration of Jesus' Public Ministry. At Tabor, *listening* imposes the necessity of obeying Jesus. The God of Sinai has now, again, made Himself apparent. Hearing, therefore, has an obedient characteristic to it. The tablets of stone are replaced by the person of Jesus.

The whiteness and brightness surrounding Jesus and emanating from Him evokes both awe and hope. The text reads: *"kai ta imatia autou egeneto stilbonta leuka lian, oia gnapheus, epi tēs gēs u dunatai outōs leukanai"* ("And the garments of Him became gleaming white exceedingly, such as fuller on the earth cannot so to whiten") (Mk 9:3). On the way down from the mountain, Jesus explained to the apostles the certainty of His degradation through the events of the Passion. Clearly, in light of the glory displayed, the love of the apostles for Jesus is certainly intentional. But the Passion of Jesus will contravene the glory that has been shown on Tabor. Nonetheless, the mandate of God charges them to obedient attention to what Jesus has to say regarding His mission.

That Jesus was now on the brink of His mission is indicated by Elijah. Jesus Himself explained: "To be sure, Elijah does come first, and restores all things. Why then is it written that the Son of Man must suffer much and be rejected? But I tell you, Elijah has come, and they have done to him everything they wished, just as it is written about him" (Mk 9:12).

The Rabbis held that Elijah *would* reappear before the day of the Messiah (Mal 4:5-6). Elijah's presence likewise recalled the tradition of the prophets and also the *fate* of the prophets. Within the Synoptic context, John the Baptist is likewise recalled as the last prophet, whose authenticity was not only not recognized but also disgraced. John's death for Salome's bidding was more humiliating than the execution itself. These signs and symbols, words and apparitions, filled Jesus' intimate friends with consternation. It is a natural reaction. Dramatic demonstrations of God's will astonish everyone.

Curiously, Mark the evangelist provided an editorial comment: "He [Peter] did not know what to say;

they were so frightened" (Mk 9:6). Peter was disoriented and awestruck. Yet, herein is a mixed metaphor. "Rabbi," he cried, meaning *my teacher.*" "Let us construct three booths here . . ." (Mk 9:5). The exhortation makes sense. In the context of Hebrew liturgy, the erection of booths indicates an enshrinement of the symbolic modes of the presence of God. It is almost as if one were to say, "This moment is too perfect, and therefore should be framed like a snapshot."

Scholars agree that Mark is Peter's own evangelist, and in his Gospel he has recorded Peter's experiences of Jesus as a major part of his overall presentation of the person of Jesus. Peter's initial reaction was that he was awestruck by what he perceived.

While Jesus is the focal point of the narrative ("Listen to Him"), the theophany of God is the staging, and the protagonist is *Peter*, then, as we have seen above, it is safe to conclude that the presentation of this important scene from the Public Life of Jesus is similar to the structure of the parables. For example, the titles of the two parables, regarding the Prodigal Son, and Lazarus and Dives, misdirect the moral of the story for the reader who comes to expect the hero to be the content of the message of the narrative. The Prodigal Son is about the father's love, not about the two boys. Lazarus and Dives is about the rich man's hardness of heart.

Here, the Transfiguration is for and about the apostles. *They* are the central figures of this incident. In the script, Peter takes the lines. The Petrine Tradition, as representative of the Church itself, is as old as the composition of the New Testament. Prior to the Tabor Event, Peter's struggle with the possibilities of Jesus' death was a prologue to the moment of the Transfiguration. The descent from Tabor, after the experience of the Transfiguration, segued into the explicitation that Jesus *had* to be put to death.

The descent included an encounter with a boy possessed by a demon. That miracle, too, addressed the inadequacy of faith. When Jesus saw the tragedy of the victim's helplessness while others tried to expel the demon, His exasperation became clear: "This is a faithless generation" (Mt 9:19).

In his Apostolic Letter, Pope John Paul II wrote that the Transfiguration is *the* Mystery of Light (*RVM*, no. 21). If Peter is the protagonist of the drama, then surely John Paul II, as the successor of Peter, would identify with the struggles and agonies of the faith of the entire Church. Yet it cannot be denied that in his own personal life, this particular Pontiff, as a twentieth-century son of Poland, had personally experienced the elements of the Passion of Jesus.

Bereft of family at an early age, he faced the nightmare years of Nazi occupation followed by Communist government. Through all those many experiences, he held to his faith tenaciously. As a man with a vision, he was full of the hope which he successfully communicated to others through many effective instruments of communication. Whether one reflects on the Mystery of the Transfiguration through the eyes of John Paul II or one's own, let it be recalled that the issues are those of faith and *hope*.

Inevitably, the Transfiguration authenticates the Christian experience as one of hesitancy, resulting from personal incomprehension, often about the presence of God in the details of one's life. Yet, according to the conventional wisdom, without such a vision of hope, the people will perish.

Throughout much of the twentieth century, now ended, preachers, theologians, and pastors have communicated the message that imitation of Christ is an expression of love for God. The idea of progress, the concurrent theme of the twentieth century, especially as evidenced by innovations in physics and biology, stated that fundamentally there is nothing wrong with human nature. It is on a steady path to success, accomplishment, and efficiency. Western society has come to expect that Christianity's role would be to remind its audience that human nature fails to appreciate God's love for humanity. It also states that Christians don't love God enough. If that were the case, progress would still be steady and certain.

Now that the twentieth century has ended, despite that progressive thinking which inaugurated it, its fruit is, in fact, the shocking evidence of human depravity. It is not necessary to recall the scenes of horror from "the human depths." Christianity was never about a new way of thinking, nor renewed efforts toward better and higher education, nor restored idealisms as representative of what is best in humanity. In this time, as in Peter's day, humanity *needs* transformation. This is God's work, and we must ask it of Him.

That is the significance of the Mystery of the Transfiguration. It is a prelude to the entire Paschal Mystery of Jesus' Passion and Resurrection, which occurred once and yet for all time. The Transfiguration is *the* light that communicates Jesus' victory over that enmity which claims to reside in the heart of creation. Jesus stood between the two figures who epitomized the Hebrew tradition, which consisted of worship, education, and the observance of the Law. He stood before the successors of Moses and Elijah, i.e., Peter, James, and John (and the College of the Apostles they represent). The Light demonstrated that the business of the marketplace, i.e., human exchange and the values of society, still presented the image of an inadequate human race.

The event evidenced to Peter and his companions that the transfiguration of all humanity was about to commence. The glory of God on Tabor was about to be transferred, not into sanctuaries made by human hands, i.e., temples of stone, like the one at Jerusalem. The presence of God would now rest, not in any tabernacle of stone, cloth, or even gold, but rather in a temple of men and women, which would be the Church.

Fifth Luminous Mystery:
The Institution of the Eucharist

FOR I received from the Lord what I also passed on to you. The Lord Jesus, on the night He was betrayed, took bread, and when He had given thanks, He broke it and said,

"This is My body, which is for you; do this in remembrance of Me." In the same way, after supper He took the cup, saying, "This cup is the New Covenant in My blood; do this, whenever you drink it, in remembrance of Me." For whenever you eat this bread and drink this cup, you proclaim the Lord's death until He comes (1 Cor 11:23-26).

There is much material for meditation when one focuses on the Mystery of the Eucharist. The three Synoptic evangelists present similar accounts of the Institution of the Eucharist, and the material can be found in Matthew 26:26-29, Mark 14:22-25, and Luke 22:17-20. St. John treats the Eucharist in another context and in another way, as part of the Public Ministry of Jesus, in that part of his Gospel known as the "Book of Signs." All of the evangelists spoke of the occasion of a "table-fellowship," and they refer to it in terms of the Feast of the Passover, i.e., that ceremonial meal which is at the heart of the Hebrew faith.

The Synoptic authors all refer to it as a Passover meal, while John places the event before the Passover (Jn 13:1). The leitmotif of John's Paschal Meal account is *love:* "Having loved His own who were in the world, He now showed them the full extent of His love" *(eis telos ēgapēsen autous*—"to the end He loved them") (Jn 13:1-3). In the Johannine context, the important word *telos*, i.e., "the end," conveys the entire message. This particular Greek word signifies bringing everything to a culminating point. *Telos* forms part of the description of a telescope. Through a telescope, the heavens are, in a way, condensed so that the heavenly bodies can be apprehended by human vision. The Paschal Supper is the summary of Jesus' motive and His mission.

In the context of the Lord's Supper, three elements stand out. The first is the bond of Jesus' affection for those who are dear to Him in the world *(Agapēsas tous idious tous en tō kosmō*—"Loving His own in the world") (Jn 13:1). John demonstrated the ineffable experience of the Last Supper by a gesture of love: Jesus bathing the feet of the Twelve. At the same time, the deed is accompanied by an explanation while Jesus was readjusting His clothing.

Jesus proclaimed Himself a teacher *(didaskalos)* who has authenticated His message by demonstrating what He wished to convey (Jn 13:14). He said: "You call me *ho didaskalos kai ho kūrios* ('the teacher and the Lord'). And rightly so, for that is what I am. Now that I, your Lord and teacher, have washed your feet, you also should wash one another's feet" (Jn 13:14). The atmosphere of love-in-service *(agape)* pervaded the event and underscored Jesus' effective use of "table-fellowship" as a unique literary form of the Bible. Rituals and gestures that represented the culture of first-century Judaism were always intended to convey what they signify.

Secondly, the word *kosmos*, i.e., "the world," formed the subtext of the Johannine narrative, as well as those of the Synoptics. According to the pattern of the entire Gospel, the Johannine structure inevitably identified the "world" with the "devil." "The evening meal was being served, and the devil had already prompted Judas Iscariot, son of Simon, to betray *(paradoi*—'to place in someone else's hands') Jesus" (Jn 13:2). The amount of money exchanged for this incredible treachery was thirty pieces of silver, or twelve dollars (Mt 27:3).

The juxtaposition of love and wickedness is likewise found in the Synoptic accounts of the Last Supper. The treachery of Satan was epitomized by the unfortunate Judas Iscariot, who *had* already succumbed to Satanic seduction. Jesus described Judas as one of the Twelve, "one who dips bread into the bowl with Me. The Son of Man will go just as it is written about Him. But woe to that man who betrays the Son of Man! It would be better for him if he had not been born" (Mk 14:20).

Mark, the earliest narrator of the Passion Account, as if to emphasize the insidious and persistent presence of the Evil One, later provided a second shock. In the scene of the arrest, Mark would report: "Going at once to Jesus, Judas said, 'Rabbi,' and kissed Him" *(katephilēsen*—"fervently kiss") (Mk 14:45). The implication appears again in the use of Rabbi as "*my* teacher." Through devices and desires, Judas has demonstrated the nature of the world where wickedness claims its place to be in the heart. Judas has shared the intimacy of the "one bowl" and has called Jesus by a title of affection, "*my* Rabbi," and he kissed Jesus intimately, according to the evidence of the New Testament Greek language, the ultimate gesture of affection.

The third element of the Lord's Supper, as the Institution of the Eucharist was called, was the breaking of bread, sharing the cup of wine, and the words of personal commitment and command, which accompanied Jesus' deeds. As recorded above from Paul's First Letter to the Corinthians, history locates the most primitive text of the Institution Account. Paul's words were probably written around the year 55 C.E. and claim that he, Paul, received this message from the Lord.

By this time, however, the information regarding the origins of the Eucharist presumably came from the primitive Church, and was passed along to Paul through the chain of first believers, who relied on the Apostles' witness. The reference to "what I received from the Lord" *(egō gar parelabon apo tou kuriou, ho kai paredōka humin, hoti ho kūrios Iēsous en tē nukti ē paredideto*—"I, for received from the Lord, what also I delivered to you, that the Lord Jesus in the night in which He was betrayed . . . ")* (1 Cor 11:23) would refer to an inner confirmation by the Holy Spirit, Who is identified with Paul's unique charism as an author of the New Testament Scriptures.

Note that Paul too has emphasized that the Eucharistic Institution occurred "*in the night in which Jesus was betrayed.*" The term "Lord" was used of Jesus after the Resurrection. The phrase, "Jesus is Lord," was the first expression of belief (Phil 2:11). The reference to Jesus as Lord in this early Eucharistic Narrative is an expression of Resurrection faith and Paul's conformity with that of the primitive Christian community. He ascribed to Jesus a royal title (Lord), indicating that Jesus was not a victim of the moment, despite the betrayal "in the night," but instead He was in charge of the events.

The Pauline Narrative here is delivered in simple and pure lines, but within the context of several specific moral directives aimed at the Church at Corinth. Paul's simplicity here, by recalling an original Eucharistic Narrative, condemned worldliness, identity with pagan rituals, self-centeredness, irreverence, and, most of all, class-consciousness. Already Paul detected signs of envy and jealousy in the Corinthian Christian community, which stemmed from the quest for prestige, a perennial theme of any human drama. Secondly, Paul was annoyed by the casual attitude with which Corinthian Christians approached the Table of the Lord.

Paul's account delineates the Institution of the Eucharist as "a mandate." "Do this, whenever you drink it, in remembrance of Me" (1 Cor 11:25). The tense of the verb is imperative. It recalls the narrative of the Transfiguration, when God the Father spoke to the apostles: "This is My Son, Whom I love. *Listen* to Him" (Mk 9:7). In the Mystery of the Transfiguration, it is the Father Who presents the command, "Listen to [obey] Him!"

In the Synoptic Eucharistic accounts, the imperative is delivered by Jesus Himself. The use of the imperative there indicates the presence of God. The juxtaposition of the two events, the Transfiguration and the Institution of the Eucharist, indicates *how* the

Christian obeys Jesus. The answer comes from identification with Jesus in the Eucharist. Further, this is an ongoing identity. One furthers and deepens an identity with Jesus at the renewal of each Eucharistic Celebration. The Institution of the Eucharist must be seen as at the heart of the work and mission of Jesus. Partaking of the Eucharist is complete identity with the total Christ.

Before the days of the Second Vatican Council, at mid-twentieth century, it had become a catch-phrase of theologians that "the Eucharist makes the Church." While the Church is associated with activities of charity, justice, evangelization, and education, the Church's principal work is the worshipful continuation of the Celebration of the Eucharist. The Eucharist magnifies the community *(koinonia)* and the works of the community *(diakonia)*. Proclamation and teaching *(kerygma* and *didache)* are also at the heart of the Church's obligation to service. Since words comfort, guide, and deliver hope, they communicate the authenticity of the whole Christ. In the Eucharistic formula are also to be found the events of Salvation History, which culminates with the Paschal Mystery.

The specific *name* given to the *Eucharist* by Scripture connotes "remembrance," "thanksgiving," and "praise." All of these concepts are identified with the Church's work of worship, as well as the devotional life of each member of the Church. The content of the Eucharistic event *must* be demonstrated in "a Liturgy after the Liturgy," to borrow an oft-used phrase of Christians from the East. Examples of generous charity, patient intervention, and Christian witness, always courageous no matter what the circumstances, are derived from the centrality of the Eucharistic Lord. Within the Eucharist, His constant affirmation of the spiritual and eternal destiny of humankind dispels the darkness of the *cosmos*. It is also the incentive to obedience to God's Will, as it applies to each of us.

The Passover Meal provides rich material for contemplation of the Eucharist, not only by a recall of the details of the Exodus as a prototype for the Eucharist. The presuppositions of Paschal prayer link the Eucharist with Hebrew culture. By re-presenting at table the details of God's mandate to Moses, the citizens of ancient Israel were of the mind that they had actually reentered the Mystery of Liberation from Pharaoh, which the words and gestures of the ritual signify. The Christian likewise believes that by contemporary participation in the Supper of the Lord, he or she actually enters into the New Covenant effected through Jesus' Death on the Cross.

Here Jesus is the new paschal lamb and the victim of the sacrifice. This is in fulfillment of the prophecies of Jeremiah: "The time is coming," declares the Lord, "when I will make a new covenant with the House of Israel and with the House of Judah" (Jer 31:31).

It is worthwhile quoting the rest of the prophecy:

"It will not be like the covenant I made with their forefathers when I took them by the hand to lead them out of Egypt, because they broke My covenant, though I was a husband to them," declares the Lord. "This is the covenant I will make with the House of Israel after that time. . . . I will put My Law in their minds and write it on their hearts. I will be their God, and they will be My people. No longer will a man teach his neighbor, or a man his brother saying, 'Know the Lord,' because they will *all* know Me, from the least of them to the greatest . . . for I will forgive their wickedness and will remember their sins no more" (Jer 31:32-34) *(emphasis, mine)*.

The prophecy of Jeremiah is extremely important to understand the Eucharist. It is the only time the Hebrew Scriptures use the phrase "The New Covenant." Jeremiah himself, the prophet's icon of the suffering servant of Isaiah, expressed with clarity the significance of the Eucharist. God was not responsible for breaking the Old Covenant. Referring to God's purity and fidelity, Jeremiah said of Him: "I was a husband," meaning "I was always faithful to you." Those who broke the covenant were faithless members of God's own people, His chosen spouse.

In the New Covenant, God again irreversibly accepts the responsibility. "This is *My* body and this is *My* blood." The first covenant was solemnized by blood from sacrificial animals. God's initiative, His responsibility, and therefore His ongoing presence are found in the New Covenant, and it is by *His* blood. The effect is that all will "know [experience] the Lord, because they will *all* know Me, from the least of them to the greatest" (Jer 31:34). This, the catholic dimension of the Eucharist as proclaimed by Paul, was foreshadowed by Jeremiah in this important prophecy. Through the Eucharist, accessibility to the presence of God is available to everybody.

There is a final note for reflection. The Eucharist contains within itself the Mystery of the Passion and Death of the Lord. From the moment that Jesus broke the bread and shared the cup with the Twelve, it was impossible for Him to turn back from His commitment to Calvary. Jesus said an irrevocable "yes" to the Will of the Father. It is inevitable, thereforc, in biblical theology that the First Eucharist be identified as a "prophetic act," i.e., an action which effects what it signifies. The Eucharist is at once Jesus' act of loving obedience to His Father and an act of communion with the brothers and sisters who are saved by Jesus' blood. To partake of the Eucharist is to participate in and to experience the effects of the saving action of Christ's love upon the Cross.

There is much food for thought regarding the Mystery of the Eucharist. With the Institution of the Eucharist, the Church *is* inaugurated. From the very earliest days of the Church, the image of the faithful, gathered around the Bishop or the priest-celebrant, recalled the everlasting banquet of heaven, where the Church is now and will be united around the Father's glory, in praise and love with the *kenosis* (generous love or outpouring) of the Son, and united through the *dunamis* ("power") (Lk 1:35). of the Holy Spirit. Careful meditation, in silence, regarding the Institution of the Rosary creates in the soul sentiments of gratitude and love for God. It is an art of arriving at an understanding of the depths of God's love. It is a process of gradualness.

By presentation of the *Luminous Mysteries of the Rosary*, Pope John Paul II has designated the Mystery of the Eucharist to be *the* central mystery of the entire Rosary. Catholic piety has consistently viewed the Rosary, because of its structure, form, and history, as a chain-link to eternity, emphasizing the events of the Incarnation and Redemption. Since the time of Pius V in the sixteenth century, the Joyful, Sorrowful, and Glorious Mysteries have provoked a sense of wonder regarding God's communication with men and women through Christ. Through focus upon the scene of the Institution of the Eucharist, the Rosary has become more precisely linked with the Prayer of the Church *now*.

The *Luminous Mysteries* deepen and develop the message of the prayer of the entire Rosary. It is Christocentric! It is celebratory, i.e., a prolonged reflection magnifying the purpose of the Liturgy! It is biblical! It is eschatological in that it is an act of praise connected with the Liturgy of the Eternal Sanctuary! In this manner, Pope John Paul II recalls the abiding presence of God, which on this limited and sometimes dark planet is the ultimate treasure of all human search.

In light of the Eucharistic reflection, the succeeding set of Mysteries of the Rosary, i.e., the Sorrowful Mysteries, become less a staging of a passion play or drama, observed by a detached third-party audience. The devotee of the Rosary is invited not to observe but to participate in the Will of the Father and the love of the Blessed Trinity as was demonstrated by the Crucified Christ.

Epilogue

IN concluding this overview, two themes present themselves. The first is the great theme of light, which inaugurated the Creation. The first sentences of the Book of Genesis reiterate the *central* theme of light to the whole of Judeo-Christian tradition. "Now the earth was formless and empty, darkness was over the surface of the deep, and the spirit of God was hovering over the waters. And God said, 'Let there be light,' and there was light. God saw that the light was good, and He separated the light from the darkness" (Gn 1:2-3). Light is associated with God Himself. Where else could God derive this first act of Creation but from within Himself?

The history and liturgy of ancient Israel have renewed the symbol of light, identifying it with the presence of God and also with new beginnings. Nowhere is this more apparent than in the Book of Nehemiah where it is recorded that the exiles had at long last returned to Jerusalem from their exile in Babylon. The priest Ezra assembled the people and began to read to them the entire Torah. He read from daybreak until noon. He began, therefore, with the first sentences of Genesis once again. By thus reading about the light, Ezra recalled Israel to its first fervor as God's people while each man, woman, and child in Jerusalem listened attentively and contemplated God's word (Neh 8:1-5).

About three hundred years before the time of the birth of Jesus, the religious party in the monastic community centered at Qumran, near the Dead Sea, evolved a theology and discipline of darkness and light. These consecrated individuals from the priestly tribe saw as their special task *to keep the vigil of the light,* lest the forces of darkness reduce the world of Jewish faith to shadows. For this, they were even prepared to fight.

In His Public Ministry, Jesus often used the image of light to speak about the interior structures of the human personality. "The eye is the lamp of the body. If your eyes are good, your whole body will be light. But if your eyes are bad, your whole body will be full of darkness. If then the light within you is darkness, *how great is that darkness?*" (Mt 6:22-23). St. Matthew's Gospel also spoke of the necessity of *vigilance* in order to keep the light burning through the responsibility for the lamp. He illustrated this with the parable of the bridesmaids. The parable only makes sense when the specifics are recalled. According to custom, the bridesmaids were charged with preparing the bride for the wedding. At night during the wedding procession, torches requiring large amounts of oil had to keep burning in order to welcome the groom and, in procession, lead the bride to the wedding chamber. The torches were long poles topped with oil-drenched rags. Because the wedding tent was outdoors, little lamps made of clay would be insignificant.

Once the bride was bathed, dressed, jeweled, scented, and veiled, the main task of the bridesmaids was to trim the torch, cutting off the ends of rags and adding oil about every fifteen minutes. The wedding light had to be kept burning until the celebration was consummated. In fact, this process required much patience and large amounts of fuel. In such a practical way, Jesus proclaimed a "Gospel of Light," specifically to bring hope, fortitude, and comfort to those who would consecrate themselves to God in the New Kingdom.

One cannot help but think of the words spoken by Pope John Paul II on his election and the inauguration of his Pontificate: "Do not be afraid!" That theme has touched every pastoral aspect of his entire Pontificate. One senses that these words were an expression of his deep and solitary personal life, which had been ripped bare by the events of his personal history. Strengthened by his experiences and his spirituality, Pope John Paul II has brought comfort to the Church throughout many uncertain days of his Pontificate.

When people do not know the future, they become afraid. Fear paralyzes! One only has to think of the experience of being alone in a strange room when the lights suddenly go out. Light brings relief, a sense of security, and the ability to forge a path into the future. The *Luminous Mysteries* stand over and against the kingdom of darkness, and are intended to both comfort and clarify as the days of the new century experience the ebb and flow of the darkness of what is yet unknown.

A second benefit of the *Luminous Mysteries* is the experience of *letting oneself be loved.* Except perhaps for the Baptism of Jesus, Peter is the constant audience of the *Luminous Mysteries of the Rosary.* The evidence of Scripture clearly indicates that Peter was an impulsive man whose bravado continually uncovered his weakness. Yet, he is the New Testament vessel of reception for Jesus' most pointed words. Peter was a man of paradox. He is capable, but inadequate. He is brave, but insecure. He is exuberant, but wretched. In short, he is like the rest of us.

In the Lucan account of the arrest of Jesus, Jesus has excoriated those who would deal with Him in terms of swords and clubs. This included Peter. "Every day I was with you in the Temple courts, and you did not lay a hand on Me. But this is your hour—when darkness reigns" *(All autē estin humōn ē hōra kai ē exousia tou skotous*—"But this is of you the hour of darkness") (Lk 22:53). Those words were the immediate prelude to the denial of Jesus by Peter.

That was Peter's hour. It was an hour of darkness. He went into the struggle of Jesus' Passion with a sense of self-sufficiency, but, like anyone prone to such an attitude, a realization of the dark moments sets in for the Christian disciple. The struggle of the Passion involved struggle for anyone associated with Jesus: Peter, John, Mary Magdalene, etc. The words *"with Me"* are of the essence of the vocation. One must not resist ominous darkness, but rather approach it with the assurance of the presence of God. This has been the perennial theme of the most beloved of our prayer traditions: "Even though I walk through the valley of the shadow of darkness, I will fear no evil, for You are with me; Your rod and Your staff will comfort me" (Ps 23:4).

In the end, after the Resurrection, Peter was interrogated on the seashore as to his love for Jesus. Peter's answer was certainly not begrudging, but he was annoyed. In the last of the three interrogations, found in St. John's Gospel (Jn 21:12-19), Jesus uses the verb for a unique form of love: *agapas/phileis me?* The first two interrogations regarding Peter's love use the word *agape,* which implies a true, committed love involving the entire personality. However, the last time the interrogation was made, the word for love implied a natural, spontaneous affection or fondness. With each interrogation, Jesus reinstated Peter and came right out to express his motive by providing him with responsibility "for furthering His mission."

The consistent presence of Peter throughout these Mysteries of the Rosary is a representation of everyone called to participate in the grace of salvation. To them, *light is love.* Within these Mysteries, Peter is the surrogate. For him, as no less for us, the ultimate expression of light is in this sentence: "Then He said to him, *'Follow Me!'* " (Jn 21:19).